Amphitheatres and Circuses

New York Clipper Building, 1869
SOUTHEAST CORNER OF CENTRE AND LEONARD STREETS

Clipper Studies in the Theatre
ISSN 0748-237X
Number Nine

Amphitheatres

.

and

Circuses

═══════

A History from Their Earliest Date to 1861

With Sketches of Some of the Principal Performers

by

Col. T. Allston Brown

Edited by William L. Slout

An Emeritus Enterprise Book
Distributed by The Borgo Press
San Bernardino, California
1994

THE BORGO PRESS

Publishers Since 1975
Post Office Box 2845
San Bernardino, CA 92406
United States of America

* * * * * * * *

Library of Congress Cataloging-in-Publication Data

Brown, T. Allston (Thomas Allston), 1836-1918.
  Amphitheatres and circuses : a history from their earliest date to 1861,
with sketches of some of the principal performers / by Col. T. Allston
Brown ; edited by William L. Slout.
    p. cm. — (Clipper studies in the theatre, ISSN 0748-237X ; no. 9)
  Appeared originally in eight installments in the theatrical columns of the
New York clipper from Dec. 22, 1860 to Feb. 9, 1861.
  "An Emeritus Enterprise Book."
  Includes index.
  ISBN 0-913960-32-2 (cloth). — ISBN 0-913960-33-0 (pbk.)
  1. Circus—United States—History. 2. Circus—History. 3. Circus per-
formers—United States. 4. Amphitheatres—United States. I. Slout, Wil-
liam L. (William Lawrence) II. New York clipper. III. Title. IV. Series.
GV1803.B76 1994   94-22302
791.3'0973—dc20   CIP

FIRST EDITION

Compiled Expressly for the *New York Clipper*
From Notes Kindly Furnished
By George Stone, an Old Professional

Col. T. Allston Brown

CONTENTS

INTRODUCTION

Col. T. Allston Brown's *A Complete History of the Amphitheatre and Circus* has been buried in the pages of the *New York Clipper* for well over one hundred years. The microfilm copies of the paper, with its small type and hazy images, is difficult to read and hard on the eyes. Although much of Brown's original text has been superseded by Stuart Thayer's immaculate research, it is still worthy of public scrutiny, for Brown was one of the original circus historians. It is with this in mind that I have set about to make this document more accessible.

The piece was first serialized in the theatrical columns of the *New York Clipper* in eight installments, running from December 22, 1860, through February 9, 1861. In this published version, we have taken the liberty, with apologies to Col. Brown, to change the title to *Amphitheatres and Circuses* for the purpose of simplification and to avoid the word "complete." Although his work could have been considered complete at the time of his writing it, later studies have added much to what we know of circus history. Therefore, we have deemed a change necessary to forestall misleading those interested in reading the book.

Much of the text of this volume is based on notes Brown obtained from George Stone. Stone, brother of the equestrian William Stone, was a clown with the various circuses of the 1830's and 1840's. From the paucity of biographical references to him, one must assume that as a jester he did not rank as high as many of his contemporaries. Thayer tells us that, during his circus career, Stone was connected with James W. Bancker, 1832; the American Circus, 1833; Aaron Turner, winter of 1833-34; Frost, Husted & Co., 1836; Eagle Circus/Cole & Co., 1837; A. Hunt & Co., 1838; Yale, Sands & Co., 1838; Miller, Yale & Howes, 1838; Charles LaForest, 1842; and Waring & Raymond, 1842.

We also know that George Stone was a native of Albany, who began his professional life at the North Pearl Street Amphitheatre under the management of Samuel Parsons. This could have been as early as 1824. As a comedian, he was said to have possessed rare dramatic talent and versatility, assets which made him particularly popular in the South and West. A friendship existed between Stone and the great American born actor, Edwin Forrest. They began their dramatic careers about the same period, although Mr. Forrest was the senior by several years. After Stone's retirement from the profession, he embarked in a commercial business in Philadelphia, where he died, December 18, 1864, in the 53rd year of his age.

"His memory," Forrest often stated, "was the most remarkable I ever knew." Scenes, faces and incidents were fully and indelibly photographed in his mind and seldom forgotten; and his visits to all the principal cities and towns of the United States and Canada in a professional capacity, and tours of England, Ireland and Scotland, afforded him ample opportunities for recording his journal, the principal portion of which was ultimately published by Henry Dickinson Stone in 1873 under the title *Theatrical Reminiscences.*

The *New York Clipper* first came into being on April 30, 1853, under the management of Harrison Fulton Trent, to serve as a sporting weekly, since daily papers did not offer detailed reporting of athletic events at that time. Consisting of four six-column pages, 14¼ by 19¼ inches and selling for 2¢ a copy, it underwent various changes in size and price throughout the remainder of the century until by 1900 it had grown to twenty-four pages with five columns per page and sold for 10¢. The original coverage included boat racing, prize fighting, baseball, pedestrianism, and even such activities as chess and checkers and a limited view of the entertainment world. When daily newspapers began paying more attention to sporting events and when the Civil War necessitated the shutting down of the popular *Spirit of the Times* because of its large circulation in the South, the *Clipper's* emphasis underwent a change to an entertainment weekly, until, practically speaking, it became the only real theatrical paper in America during the decade of 1865 to 1875. By the end of the century it was the most complete journalistic chronicler of amusements offered in this country and it continued to be until competition from *Billboard* forced its demise in 1924.

The *Clipper* was sold to Frank Queen in 1855, who, as sole proprietor and editor, soon established it as a major organ with a reputation for reliability and a sizable international readership. Francis Queen was born in Philadelphia on May 12, 1821. With only a limited formal education, he began his career as a printer's apprentice, learning the compositor's trade with the firm of Harding Brothers, Philadelphia; but he was soon forced to relinquish the job because of being nearsighted. He then opened a bookstore and circulating library on Second Street in Philadelphia, a venture inspired by his love of reading. Shortly, he sold the business to his brother, James F. Queen, and erected a large newsstand on the pavement opposite Commissioners' Hall in Southwark; but the removal of the stand was ordered (caused by an influential member of the Board of Commissioners, who apparently found it unsightly) even before it was paid for. His next venture took him to New York City, where with a small investment he opened a newsstand on the corner of Centre and Leonard Streets. The establishment consisted of a small pine table, only two by three feet in size, but large enough to display the New York daily papers. Successful operation led to a more pretentious stand under an outside stairway on the Bowery near Grand Street. This was followed by the purchase of The News Hut, 177 Bowery, from Henry Ashford. With the establishment of the new *Clipper*, he was urged by Harrison Trent to become an editor at the salary of twelve dollars a week. This appointment began an association with the paper that lasted until his death, October 18, 1882. The heirs then formed a stock company which was incorporated on March 2, 1883, as the Frank Queen Publishing Company.

Under Queen's guiding force, the *Clipper* befriended the popular amusements neglected by other publications. In addition to its dramatic interests, it became the major source for circus, Negro minstrelsy, and variety news, a position it held throughout the century. When vaudeville evolved from the old concert hall performances, the *Clipper* responded by becoming the journalistic organ for it, aiding in its development from its origins to its eventual popular and respected position in the amusement world. Through active exploitation of the theatre, circus, minstrelsy, and vaudeville, the *New York Clipper* became known to those who were a part of these branches of the business as "The Old Reliable" and "The Showman's Bible."

Col. T. Allston Brown is perhaps the most underrated amusement historian of the 19th century; but one must admit that his interest in factual material nullified an eloquence of style. He lacked the fluidity of William Dunlap, the quaintness of Joseph Ireland, and the whimsy of George C. D. Odell. But where others were primarily interested in the "higher drama," Brown concerned himself with a broader stage; and where others identified themselves with their immediate theatrical provinces, Brown kept no provincial borders. His varied experiences in the theatrical profession as literary correspondent, publisher, editor, business agent, advance man, circus treasurer, theatre manager, and talent agent supplied him with an intimate understanding of the business and its people. And the mobility required by the nature of his various employments allowed him to collect material from the innumerable cities he visited.

In addition to this particular history, Brown contributed three others to the pages of the *Clipper*. A "History of the American Stage," ran in seventeen installments from July 28 through November 17, 1860. Another and far more lengthy theatrical record began in March of 1888 as "The Theatre in America," described as "Its Rise and Its Progress During a Period of 156 Years---A Succinct History of Our First and Famous Plays and Playhouses---Opening Bills, Casts of Characters, Distinguished Actors and Actresses, Notable Debuts, Deaths, Fires, Etc., Etc." In announcing the latter, the *Clipper* editor stated:

> We speak advisedly when we say that it is the most complete---indeed, the only complete---history of the kind that has ever been written....He has been more than thirty-two years collecting the material for this stupendous work. In all that time his researches have been thorough, patient and intelligent. No historian of our stage has labored with greater enthusiasm; none who have chronicled the rise and progress of the drama in America have approached their task with a more sympathetic appreciation of its manifold perplexities and its vast possibilities.

The series served as the foundation for a work that was published in 1903, a detailed, three volume *A History of the New York Stage from the First Performance in 1732 to 1901*, which was reissued in 1964.

Brown's "Early History of Negro Minstrelsy," a painstaking documentation of "it's rise and progress in the United States," was carried by the *Clipper* in fifty-nine installments, beginning in the anniversary issue of February 17, 1912, and ending on March 8, 1914. This is the most complete record of Negro minstrelsy yet assembled. A book, also called *History of the American Stage*, was first published in 1870 and was reissued in 1969. It contains biographical sketches of members of the profession that appeared on the American stage from 1733 to 1870. The totality of these works, added to his years of contributions to the pages of the *New York Clipper*, establishes Co. T. Allston Brown as a leading historian of American amusements.

Brown was born on January 16, 1836, in Newburyport, MA, and died in Philadelphia on April 2, 1918. His grandfather was Rev. Charles William Milton, who preached in a church in that town for 42 years. Brown moved to Philadelphia in 1852 and became the Philadelphia correspondent for the *New York Clipper* in 1855 under the name of "Young Rapid." He founded the dramatic newspaper, *The Tattler*, in 1858, which was subsequently changed to *The Philadelphian*. Shortly, he became connected with the dramatic department of Col. Fitzgerald's *City Item*.

He entered the theatrical business as advance agent for the Cooper English Opera Co. in 1860. In December of that year, he was treasurer for Gardner & Madigan's Circus. While at the Front Street Theatre, Baltimore, the management had advertised for someone to ascend a tight-rope from the stage to the gallery on the back of the great Mons. Blondin. When the volunteer failed to make an appearance at the last minute, Brown undertook the piggy-back ascension himself. The next day the newspaper dubbed him "Colonel."

Col. Brown was treasurer for Madigan's Circus in the summer of 1861. The following year, he took over the business management for the Spanish danseuse and pantomimist, Isabella Cubas. In the summer of 1862, he was involved with Dan Rice's Circus and later with one bearing Tom King's name in Baltimore and Washington. Next, he was business manager for James M. Nixon when that impresario opened the Cremorne Gardens, 14th Street, NYC. In 1863, he was in advance of Hart & Simmons' Minstrels and during the summer was with Thayer & Noyes' Circus.

He became dramatic editor for the New York *Clipper* in the fall of 1863 and continued in that capacity until 1870, when he resigned to form a dramatic agency. In 1877 he managed the Theatre Comique, NYC, transferring his interest in the theatrical agency to his brother, J. Alexander Brown; but he returned to the agency business in 1878. He was again on the road managing Boucicault's "Shaugbraun," the Hanlon Brothers in "*Le Voyage en Suisse*" (having engaged them in Europe for a three-year tour of America), actress Marie Aimee, Mrs. Tom Thumb, and also Charles Arnold in "Hans the Boatman." While he was away from New York City, the dramatic agency business was taken care of by Morris Simmonds, with whom he was associated for several years.

William L. Slout

Col. T. Allston Brown's

Amphitheatres and Circuses

**A History From Their Earliest Date To 1861
With Sketches Of
Some Of The Principal Performers**

The history of amphitheatres is of considerable impor-
tance, in consequence of its connection with ancient manners.
These structures owed their origin to the barbarity of the ancients
and their ruin to the humanity of the moderns. They are the
production of Roman invention in the last ages of the republic.
The Romans were immoderately fond of every amusement of a
bloody and horrible nature. After the Samnite wars had extended
the Roman sceptre over the whole peninsula of Italy, the first
gladiatorial conflicts were exhibited in Rome in the year B.C. 260.
Lucius Metellus brought into the circus the elephants which were
part of the spoil of the Carthaginians in the year 252, and this
proved the introduction of wild beasts into the spectacles of
Rome. This soon gave birth to a profession of men denominated
gladiators, who were trained to the combat and for reward
slaughtered one another in the arena, whilst every savage animal
which the wilds of Asia or Africa produced added to the horrors of
the scene.

The first amphitheatre was constructed in a semicircular
form. Two contiguous wooden theatres, movable on wheels, were
first placed back to back and, the people being amused in these
the one half of the day, they were then wheeled round, forming
one spacious theatre, where the gladiators contended during the
remainder of the day. Julius Caesar, a few years after, formed a
hunting theatre of wood and, in consequence of the circular
position of the seats, it obtained the name of an amphitheatre.
During the reign of Tiberius, one was built at Fidenae, which,
Tacitus informs us, fell while the games were performing, killing or
injuring about 50,000 persons.

In the eighth consulate of Vespasian, he began an ·
amphitheatre which Titus finished during his reign, A.D. 80. It is
said that the expense of this building would have erected a
metropolis. Dio says that 9,000 wild beasts were destroyed at the
dedication of this huge building. During the progress of the fifth
century, these gladiatorial combats were abolished and the

amphitheatres were abandoned to the ravages of time and accident.

The amphitheatre called the Coliseum was of an elliptical form, whose largest diameter was about 581 Italian feet, and the shortest 481. The length of the diameter of the arena was about 285 feet and the breadth 182. The external circumference enclosed a *superficies* of about five acres and a half and could scarcely be included in a parallelogram of seven acres. It was capable of containing 87,000 spectators on the benches and 22,000 in the galleries. It was completed in two years and nine months, showing an astonishing instance of Roman vigor and persevering industry.

The different kinds of amusement have already been cursorily alluded to. Gladiators contended together or entered the lists with wild beasts. It appears, also, that criminals were sometimes forced to fight with these ferocious creatures for the entertainment of the people of Rome. The laws and regulations of the amphitheatre were thus: In the center sat the Emperor; the married men sat by themselves; the young men were all arranged by themselves and their tutors sat near them to observe their conduct. The attendants and servants occupied the highest gallery. The front of the gallery was assigned to the first, while the others stood behind them. At each end of the arena was a large door for the entrance and exit of men and beasts. The latter were kept in dens under the platforms and seats. On the top of the wall of the arena was a railing of iron to protect those who sat on the first platform from any sudden spring of the wild beasts.

In antiquity, a large building, either round or oval, was used among the Romans for the exhibition of chariot races and other games. Some derive the word from Circe, to whom Tertullian attributes the invention. Sassiodorus says "Circus" comes from *circuiter*. The circensian games appear to have been adopted by the Romans from the Etruscans in the earliest ages. Romulus established the games at the Circus almost as soon as [he came to] power; and the rape of the Sabines, which took place at the first exhibition of these games, probably led him to dedicate them to Census, the giver of good counsel.

The circus at first was a wooden enclosure, in which the spectators stood, a few seats being placed for the most distinguished persons. It is said that in the earliest periods of these exhibitions the goals, or terms, round which the chariots were obliged to turn, were armed with several swords, presenting their points toward the horses, thus increasing the interest to the contest by the dangers to which it was exposed. This circumstance has given rise to a singular etymology, adopted by Cassiodorus and Isidorus—*ludi circences quasi circum enses.*

The first permanent circus at Rome was built in the year B.C. 329 by Tarquinius Priscus, in the valley of Murcia, between the Aventine and the Palatine hills. It was an oblong building, without a roof, in which public chariot races and exhibitions of pugilism and wrestling took place. It was rectangular, except that one short side formed a half circle. The entrance was at the opposite end. Within, on each side of the entrance, were six arcades where the chariots stood. On both sides and on the semicircular end were the seats of the spectators, rising gradually, one above another, like steps, and resting on strong arches. At the foot of the seats there was a broad ditch, called *euripus*, to prevent the wild beasts from leaping among the spectators. Within was an open space (*arena*), covered with sand, where the games were exhibited. This space was divided lengthwise into two parts by a wall (*spina*) 12 feet thick and 6 high, adorned with little temples, altars, statues, obelisks, pyramids and conical towers. Of these last (*metae*), there were three at each end which served as goals round which the circuits were made. By the first *meta*, opposite the curved end of the circus, there were seven other pillars, with oval balls (*ova*) on their summits. One of these balls was taken down for every circuit.

On the outside, the circus was surrounded with colonnades, galleries, shops and public places. Tarquinius Priscus projected the plan of this building and some of the wealthy senators completed it. It obtained the appellation of *Circus Maximus* from its great superiority in size to those of a later date and it was for a length of time the only circus in Rome. Julius Caesar enlarged and ornamented it and it was rebuilt and richly ornamented by Augustus. Under Nero it was burnt and under Antonius pulled down. Trajan rebuilt it and Constantine made further additions to it. It is described by Dionysius of Harlicarnassus as surrounded by a portico and having numerous staircases so well distributed as to avoid any confusion of the spectators in entering or returning. Its length was 9,331½ feet and the breadth 2,187 feet. According to Aurelius Victor it was capable of containing 385,000 spectators. This great magnificence, however, was not sufficient for the successors of Augustus, since Tiberius, Caligula, Claudius and Nero all made additions to it. Of this superb edifice there only remains some intermediate vestiges on a level with the ground. Tradition has preserved its remembrance, for at Rome the place is still called *Cerchi*, which marks the site of this enormous pile, at present occupied by gardens and the cemetery of the Jews.

The circus at this time had what was called the *podium*, which was a long, open platform or passage leading quite round the edifice at an elevation of some feet from the arena of the circus. The *podium* was considered as the place of honor, into which only the principal magistrates, the pontiffs, vestals, and persons of imperial rank entered. It seems that the seats on the *podium* were not permanent, since it was the privilege of those who had places there to send their magisterial chairs.

The great circuses, as well as the theatres and amphi-theatres, were divided into several ranges of seats for the purpose of placing the spectators according to their condition. The ranks of seats were called *maeniana*, and of course there were as many precinctions and ambulatries as ranks of seats. To maintain order in such a concourse of people as attended the exhibition, there were persons called designators, who were to assign to every one his place, that there might be no mixture of persons of different ranks, a point in which Roman pride was very jealous. All the seats were covered with wood, which circumstance accounts for the fires which are mentioned to have happened in these edifices. It was also customary for women to bring cushions and stools to place their feet upon. The area of the circus was of earth, but probably beaten. Caligula and Nero carried the extravagant luxury so far as to cover the area with *chrysocolla* and *minium*, disposed in regular figures.

The games exhibited in the circus were celebrated regularly on certain fixed days and were named from various deities as Apollo, Flora, Ceres, Saturn, Consus, Bacchus, etc. They were more or less magnificent. According to the ritual, some were celebrated only once in a century and were therefore called secular. Some were instituted for the birthday of the emperor; others for every *lustrum*, which were called *vota quinquenralia*. The games sometimes lasted for several days. There were public funds appropriated to defray the expenses but they were frequently given by individuals who aspired to popular favor. Till the time of the elder Tarquin, they were held on an island of the Tiber and were called Roman games. After that prince had built the Circus, they took their name therefrom, as being constantly held there.

The following were the exercises in the arena: A splendid procession opened the festival, after having marched through all the principal streets of the city. The chief magistrate led the procession. Before him was carried the image of the winged goddess of Fortune (*Fortunata Plata*). Then came the images of Jupiter, Juno, Minerva, Neptune, Apollo, Diana. After the death of Julius Caesar, his image was introduced. These images were in splendid covered chariots, drawn by horses or mules, stags, camels, elephants, also sometimes by lions, panthers or tigers. After the pompous procession of gods, followed rows of boys who had lost either father or mother, and who led the horses to be used in the races. After these, followed the sons of the patricians, from fifteen to sixteen years of age, armed, part on horseback, part on foot. After these came the magistrates of the city and the senate. The sons of knights, on horseback and on foot, brought up the rear. Then followed the chariots and horses destined for the races and the different *athletae*, as pugilists, wrestlers, runners, all naked except a covering about the loins. In this procession were included the dancers, youths and boys, arranged in rows, according to their age. They wore violet colored garments with brass belts and carried swords and short spears. The men wore helmets. Each division was preceded by a man who led the windings of the dance. The musicians followed, including a number of persons dressed like Sileni and Satyrs; who, with large wreaths of flowers in their hands, exhibited various sportive dances, with a company of musicians behind them. To this exhibition of wild, unrestrained joy, succeeded the religious pomp. First came the *camilli*—boys whom the priests employed in the sacrifices—then the servants who took part in it. After these, the *haruspices* with their knives; and the butchers who led the victims to the altar; the different orders of priests with their servants---first, the high priest (*pontifex Maximus*) and the other *pontifices*, then the *flamines*, then the *augurs*, the *quindecim viri* with the Sybilline books; the vestal virgins; then the remaining inferior orders of priests according to their rank. The images of the gods brought up the rear; sometimes, also, a pompous show of treasure, the spoils of war.

In the Circus, the procession went round once in a circle and the sacrifices were then performed. The spectators took their places, the music struck up, and the games commenced. These were, first, races with horses and chariots (These were so honorable that men of the highest rank engaged in them); second, wrestling and fighting with swords, staves and pikes; third, Saltatic dancing; fourth, *disci*, quoits, arrows and *certes*, all which were on foot; fifth was horse coursing; the sixth, course of chariots, whether with two horses or with four.

Each exhibition consisted of twenty-five courses and each course of four chariots; thus the whole number of chariots required was one hundred. The chariots had at first only two horses and were called *bigoe*. In process of time, there was added another horse, which was called *funarius* because he was attached to the car by a rope. At length, one more was added and the car became *quadrida*, which was the most general practice. But sometimes the directors of the game added to each car a fifth horse with a rider; and, in the inscription relating to Diocles, there are even mentioned six and seven horses abreast.

The light cars used in these games had two wheels and were nearly balanced upon the axle. The front, which was circular, had a kind of parapet about the height of the driver's knee. The charioteer mounted behind and stood upon the floor of the chariot. All the horses used had their tails cut short and they were so accustomed to the contest that they often ran without the whip. Pliny relates that once, a charioteer having fallen from his car, the horses performed the course in the usual manner and gained the palm.

The drivers were generally slaves, though sometimes persons of rank and fortune exercised this art for amusement. They wore a round helmet, fastened under the chin, to defend their heads in case of a fall. A crooked knife, stuck among the belts, was an essential part of their equipment; for as the reins were fastened around the middle of the driver, he would, if he happened to fall from his chariot, have been killed by being dragged around the circle if he had not the means of cutting the reins. A white chalk line was drawn across the circus to mark the beginning and the termination of the course. The charioteers were permitted to clash with and overturn their adversaries, provided it did not happen before they entered the course. The victor obtained a palm and, in later times, a crown. He was called *bravium*, which term is apparently the origin of bravo and brave in modern languages. The spectators frequently remained whole nights and days in the circus, exposed to the weather and without leaving their places to take any refreshments. The expense of the games was often immense. Pompey, in his second consulship, brought forward 500 lions at one combat of wild beasts; which, with eighteen elephants, were slain in five days. There was also a representation of naval engagements (*naumachioe*), for which purpose the circus could be laid under water.

II

During the reign of King Charles the Second, a Mr. James Hall flourished as a rope dancer and, according to all accounts, he was the finest specimen of the human form then in England. He was admired alike for the symmetry and elegance of his figure and for his strength and agility. In the exercise of his art he exhibited the powers of a Hercules, while in his person were displayed the charms of an Adonis. Hall is said to have rivaled his Sovereign in the affections of the famous Duchess of Cleveland, from whom he received a regular salary. The wits of the time made the most of this tender liaison and many a song and lampoon, of which it was the fruitful subject, redounded much more to the honor of the rope dancer than to that of her Grace. But such things were common in that profligate's reign and the reader will not be surprised to learn that, notwithstanding the notoriety of this intercourse between Hall and the royal favorite, his majesty was so blind to her faults that, to him at least, she only appeared still more handsome. Pope has some caustic lines in allusion to this subject in his "Sober Advice from Horace."

The first exhibition of tight rope performances took place in Philadelphia on what was then called Society Hill in the year 1724. A booth was erected and the show continued in that location for a few days. The performers were a woman and a boy, whose names are not given in the programs. The exhibition was not of a high order of merit. The "boy capered on the tight rope." The woman danced on the same elastic cord with baskets tied to her feet, and she walked upon the same insubstantial path trundling a wheelbarrow before her.

As early as 1771, equestrian performances were given in Centre Square, Philadelphia, where a tent was pitched under the management of one Faulks. As ring exercises were then uncommon, Mr. F. thought it judicious to give a detailed description of his feats. The following was the program of his final exhibition:

Mr. Faulks intends presenting his feats in horsemanship for the benefit of the prisoners confined in the gaol of the city.

1. He mounts a single horse, standing in the saddle, and rides him, playing the French horn.

2. He mounts two horses, one foot in each horses stirrup, putting them into full speed, throwing himself upon his back, managing them in the same manner as if he had the advantage of a common seat, and rises again, all on the same spot.

3. He mounts three in the saddle, and rides them in full speed, vaulting from one to the other.

4. He concludes his performance by riding on a single horse at full speed, dismounting and mounting many times, and will, in that stretch, dismount freely with both feet on the ground, vault clear over the horse, back again, and mount on the "near side."

These feats were much inferior to those which we see in the circus at the present day but they must have excited a great stir among our ante-revolutionary inhabitants.

In September, 1772, one Bates, an equestrian, visited Philadelphia and opened at Centre Square. There were no night exhibitions and about dusk the equestrian ceased and the audience dispersed. After giving several exhibitions, Mr. B. concluded with a charity performance, in imitation of his illustrious predecessor, Faulks, on the 4th of November, 1772. The following was the program:

TO THE PUBLIC

Mr. Bates intending in a short time to leave the Province, and being desirous of manifesting his gratitude to this city, proposes to exhibit on Thursday next, all his various feats in HORSEMANSHIP, having confidence in the general attendance of the citizens, as the sum which may then be collected shall be deposited in the Hands of three Gentlemen of Reputation, who will apply it, in the advancing inclement season, to the relief of such modest poor as have experienced better days. The doors to be opened at three o'clock, and to mount precisely at four.

Centre Square was on the south side of Market Street, between Schuylkill, Seventh and Eighth Streets. Here, August 15th, 1785, was erected the first circus which was built in Philadelphia. One Poole, an American equestrian, was the adventurer. Among his performances was the introduction of three horses, who laid themselves down as if dead; one would groan, apparently through extreme sickness and pain; afterwards rise and make his manners to the ladies and gentlemen. Another having laid down for a considerable time, would rise and set up like a lady's lap dog.

Tickets for the first seats at five shillings, and for the second, three shillings and ninepence each, may be had at the two coffee houses. N.B.---Mr. Poole beseeches the ladies and gentlemen who honor him with their presence to bring no dogs with them.

In 1787 the circus was used by Bates as a riding school. Poole claimed the distinction of being "the first American who ever exhibited feats of equestrianism on the continent."

In the year 1792, Mr. John B. Ricketts arrived in Philadelphia from Scotland and erected a circus at the southwest corner of Twelfth and Market Streets. It opened on the 22nd of October and was at first designed as a riding school. The establishment was conducted for this purpose during the ensuing fall and winter but Mr. R. determined to erect a better building for public exhibitions.

The new establishment was fitted up on the same spot with accommodations for about eight hundred persons. The doors opened at three o'clock in the afternoon and the exhibitions were given by daylight. Ricketts was a pupil of the great Hughes, manager of the circus near Blackfriars' Bridge, London. He [Ricketts] opened on Wednesday, April 3rd, 1793. Performances were given three times a week. He was soon joined by Sig. Spinacuta, a tight rope dancer and pyrotechnist; also a brother, Master Francis Ricketts, who was afterwards an excellent rider and tumbler. He trained a boy by the name of Strobach to ride on his shoulders as a flying Mercury. General Washington attended the exhibition on the 22nd of April and gave the benefit of his presence as a guarantee of its respectability. On the 22nd of July, 1793, the season closed with a benefit to the distressed emigrants from Cape Francois, who were then in the city. The following was the advertisement:

Mr. Ricketts is desirous to announce to the ladies and gentlemen of Philadelphia his most grateful and sincere acknowledgments for the extraordinary encouragement which they have conferred on him since his arrival in this city. His departure for New York is fixed for Monday next and his return will be within the space of a few months. In the meanwhile, as there are a number of outstanding tickets, Mr. Ricketts means to give one other opportunity for them to come in and has therefore resolved on an EXTRAORDINARY PERFORMANCE THIS DAY. Particulars will be mentioned in the bills of the day. Should any tickets still be outstanding, Mr. Ricketts will be much obliged to those who hold them, either to visit the circus this day or to send them to Mr. Bradford's, where, if required, the money will be returned.

On the 11th, Spinacuta took a benefit. I present a copy of his bill to show the order of entertainments offered in those days:

Ricketts' Equestrian Circus.

Spinacuta's Benefit.

Tomorrow, the 11th of July, 1793, Mr. Spinacuta, ever studious to render the amusements on his benefit truly splendid as well as pleasing, will, in the course of the performance (for that day only) particularly distinguish himself by a variety of new Performances, in the serious and comic line.

Tight Rope. Part I. Dances on the rope with baskets fixed to his feet. An elegant hornpipe in a variety of steps. Without the assistance of the Balance pole, he will put half a crown on his foot, throw it in the air, and catch it in a glass. Several favorite airs, with variations, on the Violin.

Part II. Horsemanship. Great feats of horsemanship, entirely new, by Mr. Ricketts, Master Ricketts, Master Strobach, and Mr. McDonald, Clown to the Equestrian Performance.

Rope Dancing. A Comic Dance on the Tight Rope, with Skates. (This feat was never performed by any in America.) Sitting on a chair, he will balance a table before him and drink off a glass of wine; the whole of this performance on the plank. The surprising Leap over the Garter, Backwards and forwards, upwards of 14 feet high. Several maneuvers with the Hoop and Cane, as also with the Flag. Great feats by Mr. Ricketts. The whole to conclude with THE TAILOR Riding to Brentford Election.

Tickets sold at Mr. Bradford's Book Store, Mr. Story's, and at the Circus. The doors will be opened half an hour sooner than usual, viz: exactly at 5 o'clock, and the performance begins at 6 o'clock.

Ricketts then visited New York, where he remained two months. Returning to Philadelphia, he commenced his season on the 20th of September, 1794. He announced a full brass band as having been engaged, which would discourse most excellent music. He also printed the following in the papers of the day:

Mr. Ricketts having lately introduced a new scene at the Circus, of the "Sailor's Fox Hunting Voyage," it may afford some amusement to our readers to be informed of the particulars.

The jolly tar enters by hailing the ship, "aboard ship, ahoy." The master of a riding school appears and asks, "What's your will, sir?"

Sailor. "Are you the master of this here vessel?"

Master. "I am the master of the riding school."

Sailor. "O! your most obedient, Mr. Master. Pray, sir, do you learn gentlemen to ride? You must know that about three months ago I went down into the country to see my father, when being hailed by an old shipmate, he asked me to take a voyage of fox hunting, which I told him I would. He ordered the swabber to rig me a horse, which he did and brought me. I climbed up the side-ladder and threw myself across him thus. No sooner had I got seated than we piped all hands to get the fox out of the hole. He no sooner got out than he bore away. We crowded all the sail we could to keep up with him, but I, not knowing how to steer my horse, happened to port my helm instead of weathering it. I, at the same instant, came bump ashore against the stump of an old tree, unshipped my knee-pan, and was obliged for three weeks to go upon jury masts."

Master. "By your figure and dress, sir, it don't appear to me that you have any business to mount a horse at all."

Sailor. "My dress, sir! what have you say to my dress? Give me leave to tell you, there are more honest hearts under sailors' jackets than you are aware of. But that's nothing to the purpose. Pray what do you charge for half a dozen lessons? For as I was walking down the docks I heard as how you was the best reformer of awkward horsemen, and I made the best of my way to find you out."

Master. "Well, sir, since it is your wish, my charge is a dollar a lesson."

Sailor. "Well, come, there's six dollars; let me have the half dozen lessons at once."

After the above dialogue, a number of seafaring phrases take place whilst the sailor is getting instructions, and he makes several curious attempts at horsemanship, but at length arrives at that degree of perfection that he can dance a hornpipe as well as Mr. Ricketts, on horseback. The night, however, being rather cool, he calls for an old canvas cloak or sack, into which he is conveyed, and rides snug from the weather for a few glasses; presently the sack is carried away in a storm and the honest tar is metamorphosed into a smart lady, with her fan and fine dress, galloping two horses, Jehu-like, around the Circus.

The effect of this scene is always extremely agreeable. We hear it is to be performed for the last time this day, as Mr. Ricketts' stay will be but short in Philadelphia.

Having resolved to erect a more substantial place of amusement and one more fitted to the citizens, he closed this establishment on the 12th of November of the same year.

Ricketts once more bent his steps towards New York, where a circus was erected in Greenwich Street; and he continued to delight the citizens of that city until the following October. Returning to Philadelphia, he opened on the 19th of October, 1795, his new amphitheatre, located at the corner of Chestnut and Sixth Streets. The house was of a circular form and 97 feet in diameter. The walls were 18 feet high, from which sprung the roof in a conical shape to the height of 50 feet, being decorated at the apex with a figure of a flying Mercury. There were three entrances, the principal one being on Chestnut Street through a handsome portico. The stage was at the south end of the building and, though small, it was adapted to dramatic performances. The shape of the interior was that of a horse shoe. The ring was in the pit and in front of the stage. The house held from twelve to fourteen hundred persons. On the opening night, the house was crowded. I present a copy of the bill to show the strength of the company:

New Amphitheatre will be opened on Monday, 19th inst. Equestrian performances by Mr. Ricketts, Mr. F. Ricketts, Master Long, and Mr. Sully, Clown to the Horsemanship, his first appearance in this city. Unparalleled feats in Lofty Tumbling. Principal Performers: Mr. Sully, Master Sully, Master Long, and Mr. F. Ricketts. Clown, Sig. Reano. Slack Rope Dance by Sig. Reano. Boxes One Dollar; Pit Half a Dollar. No person admitted behind the scenes. Days of performance Monday, Wednesday, Thursday and Saturday.

At his benefit, F. Ricketts rode on his head, balancing himself on a pint pot, the horse at full speed. Mr. Ricketts sometimes rode on two horses, standing on a great mug placed loosely on each steed. His horse, Complanter, had been so admirably trained that he nightly leaped over another horse fourteen hands high and nearly as tall as Complanter. This was considered a wonderful thing and drew crowds to the amphitheatre. During the season, pantomimes were produced. The season here closed April 23rd, 1796, having first, in accordance with his usual custom, given the proceeds of one night's performance for the benefit of the poor.

III

On the 17th of September, 1794, Messrs. Ambroise & Co. opened an amphitheatre in Philadelphia. It was situated in Arch Street, between Eighth and Ninth. [There was] a representation of taking the Bastille, in which the shattering of the drawbridge was fearfully depicted and balls were "seen issuing from the cannons and musketry."

October 30th, 1796, Ricketts opened his place as the "Pantheon and Amphitheatre." The company was adapted for dramatic as well as equestrian performances. On the 18th of February, 1797, Ricketts closed the season and bent his steps towards New York, where he performed for a time in Greenwich Street. In July he visited Lower Canada, where he met with great success. Returning to New York, December, 1798, he played two weeks.

In February, 1798, a lot was secured at the northwest corner of Fifth and Prune Streets. The establishment was erected on a scale of grandeur hitherto unknown in Philadelphia. From Fifth Street it extended westward along Prune Street to the jail wall; half a square in depth. Along Fifth Street the front extended to the south wall of the present boundary of St. Thomas' Church. This remarkable building was tenanted professionally by the most splendid and well-appointed double company which had ever come to America; in which were also included some who had hitherto been attached to Ricketts' troupe. The equestrians were Messrs. Langley, Sully, Herman, McDonald, Lailson, Vander-velde, Kearns, and Miss Vanice (The first female equestrian who ever appeared in America.). The dramatic, operatic and panto-mimic performers were numerous. Lialson was the manager. The opening night was April 8th, 1798, with equestrian exercises and pantomime of "*Les Quatre fils ay Mons.*" The company was far superior to any which had yet visited the country but it was too expensive. They were composed mainly of French people, who were unable to perform in pieces suitable to the tastes of the company. The season closed August 1st.

During the ensuing winter, Ricketts' theatre was occupied by Ambroise & Co., who gave exhibitions of five weeks there.

On the 8th of March, 1798, Lailson again opened his amphitheatre with the following company: Sig. Francisguy, Lapointe, Tompkins, Louisier, Gaetan, Glaive, Miss Lailson, Mrs. Rowson, Mrs. Tompkins, Madame Corre, Miss Robinson, Miss Donvilliers, Miss Tessiere, Mrs. Bonneau, Mons. Donvilliers, Mons. D'Estinoal, Mrs. Tompkins, Mrs. Harwood, Miss Vanice, Mons. Lailson, Sully, Herman, Langley, etc.

The season closed the middle of June. The enterprise was too expensive and poor Lailson was reduced to a situation of great distress. He pledged and sold all his horses and dresses to get himself and his company to France. Some of the corps remained; others went to the French West Indies. Sully and Mrs. Rowson opened at Ricketts', where they performed for a few nights. The equestrians fitted up the old riding school at Twelfth and Market Streets as the Federal Summer Circus. In the company were Herman, Tompkins, Sully, Miss Lailson, Miss Vanice.

The finale of Mons. Lailson's equestrian adventure in Philadelphia happened about a month after the closing of the amphitheatre. On Sunday morning, July 8th, 1798, the immense dome gave way and fell to the ground between the walls, crushing the interior completely. The circus had been occupied during the preceding week by McPherson's Blues as a place of exercise.

Ricketts returned to Philadelphia and opened the season at Sixth and Chestnut, December 26th, 1798. John B. Ricketts, the proprietor, was a very gentlemanly and neat fellow in society and dressed in rather the English sporting style and was received with favor in the best circles. As a performer he never offended the eye by ungraceful postures or by the nude style of dressing that now prevails at the circus. His costumes were like that of the actors on the stage---pantalets, trunks full disposed, and neat cut jacket---which were sufficient to make ample display of his figure for all purposes of agility and grace. He would throw a somersault over twelve or fourteen files of men with fixed bayonets at a shoulder. The season closed about the beginning of April.

On the 21st of November, 1799, Ricketts again opened his amphitheatre. The season was very successful up to the 17th of December, when it was destroyed by fire. The pantomime announced for the evening was "Don Juan," with the following cast: Don Juan, Mr. Durang; Don Ferdinand, Mr. Ricketts; Commandant, Mr. Lewis; Landlord, Mr. Rowson; Scaramouch, F. Ricketts; Pedro, Mr. Hutchins; Fisherman, Herman; Donna Anna, Mrs. Rowson; Confidante, Mrs. McDonald; Fisherwomen, with a duet, Mrs. Doctor and Mrs. Rowson. The play bill contained the following announcement:

> The last scene represents the infernal regions, with a view of the mouth of hell. Don Juan, being reduced by his wickedness to the dreadful necessity of leaping headlong into the gaping gulf in a shower of fire amongst the furies, who receive him on the points of their burning spears and hurl him at once into the bottomless pit.

This announcement, which was so terrific in itself, had much to do with the subsequent reports concerning the destruction of the building. It was ascertained that a drunken carpenter, having occasion to go into a loft belonging to the building in which old scenery was stored, set the candle down carelessly near the roof and staggered away, leaving the light burning. In a short time the building was in a blaze. The audience vacated the building in safety. Ricketts lost about $20,000 and was in fact broken up completely....

In 1806, Messrs. Pepin, Breschard and Cayetano's circus arrived in Boston. They left Paris for Madrid and then sailed for the United States. Victor Pepin was born in Albany, N.Y., but when quite young his parents removed to France, where he was educated. Breschard and Cayetano were Frenchmen.

In 1809, Pepin & Breschard erected an amphitheatre at the corner of Ninth and Walnut Streets, Philadelphia (now known all over the United States as the Walnut Street Theatre and under the very able management of Mrs. Garrettson, a lady who has done much to advance the interests of the drama in that city). It commenced in March, 1808, and was opened by the above managers on February 2, 1809. Their company was numerous and well appointed. Their stud of horses was thoroughly broken and composed of splendid animals. Their wardrobe was new, costly and, indeed, the best thing of the kind that had been seen in the country. Horses, riders, and all appurtenances were brought with them from Spain. The present stage of this theatre was not erected until two years after the circus was opened. The same walls are now standing, with the exception of the front on Walnut Street, which was entirely rebuilt from designs by Haviland in 1828.

Pepin & Breschard played to fine houses. Pepin was a dashing rider, executing surprising leaps over an illuminated gallery without that eternal dodging of the object over which the rider leaps, which we witness nowadays with the garters or the canvas. I have not seen a more dexterous or sure equestrian since Pepin.

In 1811, Messrs. Pepin & Breschard connected themselves with Mr. Beaumont, the actor, and under their joint management opened the Baltimore Olympic Circus on the 6th of November. The opening night, there were four hundred dollars in the house. The piece played was "Lovers' Vows." Noticing the opening night, an editor of one of the city papers remarked that "this project of uniting theatrical with equestrian performances may lead to the most dangerous perversion of an amusement, which in its proper form is both dignified and instructive." The opening bill was as follows:

"LOVERS VOWS."

Baron Wildenheim, Mr. McKenzie; Count Carrel, Webster; Anhalt, Allen; Frederic, Beaumont; Verdun, Mestayer (one of the riders); Landlord, Thornton; Cottager, Wilmot; Poor Farmer, Roberts; Rich Farmer, Jacobs; Agatha Friburgh, Mrs. Bray (formerly Miss Murdon); Amelia, Mrs. Wilmot; Cottager's Wife, Mrs. Mestayer; Country Girl, Thornton. After which "A grand display of horsemanship and fireworks." The prices of admission are one dollar for the boxes, and half a dollar for the pit. The curtain rises at half past six.

Soon after, the Messrs. P. & B. erected a frame circus in Anthony Street, New York. Large sums of money were made by these managers, even with a limited population. The performances were so attractive, the riding so graceful, that all the taste and fashion of the city crowded the circus to the evident injury of the legitimate drama; and, finally, the Park Theatre managers themselves opened a circus at Tattersall's.

In 1816, Pepin & Breschard returned to Philadelphia and, on the 19th of August, opened the Olympic Theatre as a circus. The following persons were in the company: Pepin, Garcia, Menial the Clown, Wilson, Dusolle, W. Knappe, Williams, Harris, Robinson, Master Coty, Master Thomas, Mrs. Wilkins, Mrs. Williams, and Mrs. Wilson. In a short time the following additions were made to the company: F. Durang, Welsh, Phillips, Bradberry, Mrs. Gilbert, Mrs. Crane, and Mrs. Hewett.

In November, 1816, T. West, the equestrian, arrived in New York in the ship Chancey, Capt. Dondell, after a passage of forty-four days, with his celebrated circus corps, stage performers, and a splendid stud of colored horses. On the voyage they were obliged to throw overboard several valuable horses. The weather was very rough. West was immediately engaged by Pepin & Co. and they opened in Philadelphia on November 28th for twelve nights. The animals were the first spotted horses ever seen in this country. In the company were Campbell (clown), Walter Williams, William Williams and wife, Lawson, Rogers, Yeaman, Blackmore, and Mrs. West. This corps first introduced here the exercise of still vaulting with the springboard, wherein Campbell used to execute many novel and amusing feats. On the 19th of December the melodrama of "Timour the Tartar" was produced here. The piece was well put upon the stage; ramparts were scaled by the horses and breaches were dashed into. In the last scene, where Zorilda, mounted on her splendid white charger, ran up the stupendous cataract to the very height of the stage, the feat really astonished the audience, who rose with a simultaneous impulse to their feet and with canes, hands and wild screams kept the house in one uproar of shouts for at least ten minutes.

After a very successful season, the Olympic closed January 4th, 1817. West, with Pepin & Co., went to Baltimore and from there to New York, where "Timour" and "The Cataract of the Ganges" met with unprecedented success. This company made a tour of the United States, visiting nearly all the principal cities and making for the manager quite an independence. [West] finally sold out his establishment to Price & Simpson of the Park Theatre and Mr. Joe Cowell was the manager. In his reminiscences, Mr. Cowell says:

> West, with a fine company of performers and a magnificent stud of horses, paid a yearly visit to New York to the serious injury to the theatre; and, in self defense, Price & Simpson were desirous to buy him out. To effect this, resort was had to stratagem, in which I played a very useful part. My particular intimacy with the management being notorious, with binding oaths of secrecy, I named to those well fitted to instantly convey the news to West that the Park proprietors intended erecting a most splendid amphitheatre in Broadway, on the vacant lot where the Masonic Hall now stands. A model somewhat after the plan of Astley's was placed in the green room and imagination, aided by the whisper abroad, soon gave it a local habitation and a name. A delinquent from the circus (Tatnall) was engaged and employed to break two horses in a temporary ring, boarded around, in a lot on the alley at the back of the theatre. These broad hints at opposition soon brought matters to an issue and at a fair price and easy mode of payment; for a large portion of the amount was raised by the receipts after they were in possession. Simpson and Price and some others who then objected to be known to be interested...purchased the buildings, lease, engagements, horses, wardrobe, scenery, and a prohibition against West again establishing a circus in the United States; and, well

pleased with such a winding up to his experiment, West, with a handsome
fortune, went to England.

On the 14th of July, 1823, Cowell assumed the management of this circus company. Large additions to horse and foot
were made and the company was both extensive and excellent,
[with] a stud of thirty-three horses, four ponies and a jackass,
which, for beauty and utility, could not be equaled. They started
on a circuit, visiting Boston, Philadelphia, Baltimore, Washington
and Charleston. At the last named place, a large building had
been erected, but without a stage, and Blythe had been already
sent there with an exclusively equestrian company to perform
during the winter months. Eighteen of the most valuable horses
and fifty-five ponies, including musicians, artists and carpenters,
were selected by Cowell, who set off for the sunny South in the
ship Orbit, Capt. Fish. One thousand dollars was paid for the use
of the vessel, furnishing their own bedding and provisions and
fitting up at their own expense, the stables upon deck and the
temporary berths and state rooms between. It was in the month
of January on a fine, sun-shiny Sabbath morning that they hauled
out from the wharf at Baltimore. There was not a breath of air
stirring nor a ripple on the water to disturb the equanimity of man
or horse---a calm so profound as to realize the immortal Donne's
beautiful illustration: "In one place lay feathers and dust, today
and yesterday."

During the passage, a heavy storm arose and for five
days, with the ship hove to all the time, they experienced a fearful
gale. After a passage of fifteen days, they reached Charleston,
S.C., with the loss of a deck-load of horses. All the horses died
from hurts and bruises received during the gale and were cast
overboard. The horses were most imprudently stalled on the spar
deck instead of between decks. The sea made a complete breach
over them, literally drowning them; and the falling spars made
deep gashes in their flesh and broke their limbs.

In 1817, Messrs. James Caldwell and James Entwistle,
with Pepin's equestrian company being thus united, acted through
the winter of 1817-18 in the District of Columbia, commencing the
season at Alexandria. Visiting Philadelphia, they opened the
Olympic, April 16, 1818, which night introduced to a Philadelphia audience Mr. James H. Caldwell in the character of

"Three Singles." After a laborious season, the company moved to Baltimore. The circus stood in Old Town in one of the cross streets leading to Fell's Point. It was a huge frame building and in ruins. On the 6th of June, 1818, the equestrian department dissolved from the dramatic corps. The Olympic continued open as a circus only, under the management of Pepin, until June 13th.

Entwistle and Pepin entered into an arrangement to re-open the Olympic in the autumn. Entwistle went to England to engage talent. The Olympic Circus, corner of Ninth and Walnut Streets, Philadelphia, commenced its second campaign, under the new lessees, May 1st, 1823; George Blythe, formerly director at Astley's Royal Amphitheatre, Westminster Bridge, London, was engaged by Stephen Price as ring director and general manager. The following were the company: Messrs. Hunter, Yeaman, Tatnall, Walter Williams (clown); Masters Turner, LaForest, Whittaker and Sweet; riding master, William Lawson; Asten was vaulter and trampoline performer, afterwards ringmaster; Mrs. Tatnall, Mrs. Parker, Mrs. Carnes, Mrs. Monier, Mrs. Honey, etc. Turner made his debut here this season. The season closed May 30th with a grand benefit to George Blythe, when the grand equestrian melodrama, "El Hyder," was produced for the second time.

The season of 1825 at the Olympic opened May 1st. Messrs. Whittaker, Sweet and Spencer were in the company and were making rapid progress in their profession. Hunter was the bareback rider, much to the delight of the gallery boys. Stoker was the performer on the slack rope. The season closed on the 27th of the month and they proceeded to Baltimore and Washington.

On the 29th of August, Joe Cowell opened the Olympic for the fall season. In the equestrian troupe were Hunter, Stoker, Rogers, S. Stickney, Hunt, Sweet, Whittaker, Davis, Parker, Asten, Blakely, Lee, Gullen, Lessford, Jamie, Williams (clown), Blythe (ringmaster), and Mrs. Williams, female equestrian. James Kirby, the celebrated clown from Drury Lane, was engaged.

On the 15th of April, 1826, Tatnall and several other equestrians and actors converted Tivoli Garden, Philadelphia, into a circus and theatre and called it Pavillion Circus. Among the equestrian corps, I find Green (a two-horse rider), Tatnall,

Florence, James Bancker, Miller, Davis, Hughes (clown), Maxey, Mrs. Tatnall. Master Turner, the celebrated American equestrian, made his appearance on the first of May and performed wonderful feats, throwing back somersaults from the horse and alighting on the steed's back. I have never seen it equaled except by Master James Madigan. Our friend, Sam Tatnall, jealous of the success of Master Turner, attempted to outvie him in his performances; the consequence was, Tatnall broke his leg, which proved his last performance amid the sawdust. On the 10th of June this house closed.

The Olympic opened August 7th for the season of 1826, under the management of Joe Cowell. The company was as follows: George Blythe (ringmaster), Messrs. Buckley, Spencer, Stoker, Master Sweet, and Collet. Mr. Buckley, a very clever clown from Astley's Amphitheatre, London, made his debut on the opening night. The season closed on the 2nd of December. William Dinneford and George Blythe were then appointed by Simpson as managers of the circus. Cowell assumed the management of the Philadelphia Theatre.

IV

In the autumn of 1826, General E. W. Sandford, Esq., erected in Grand Street, New York, the Mount Pitt Circus. It was built of wood, with the exception of a brick front. It was remarkable for nothing but its bulk, being calculated to contain from 3,000 to 4,000 persons. The left wing was occupied in front as a porter room and in the rear as a stable. When opened, it was known as the Lafayette. With every horse that could be purchased with a long tail and a spot in its neighborhood, a few runaway members of Cowell's company, with Tatnall at their head and a few boys whose "vaulting ambition" had rendered them superior in gymnastic talent to any that could be produced in Europe, he commenced his campaign with Watkins Burroughs, from the Surrey and Adelphi Theatres, to conduct the dramatic department. This concern was not a paying one and it ultimately brought the proprietor to a state of bankruptcy. On a certain occasion "El Hyder" was to be produced. The part of Harvey Clifton belonged to Mrs. Tatnall, who had played it exceedingly well. When the benefit night of Mrs. Pelby (who was exclusively an equestrian) came, that lady thought it would be an attraction for her to undertake the part. She received the consent of the stage manager and, in consequence, Mrs. Tatnall was furious and vowed to be revenged. The part is that of a dashing young midshipman, after the true Sadler's Wells model, in white tights, fighting broadsword combats to no particular tune, with three or four giant-like assassins at a time; shouting for "liberty" at the end of every speech, "dam' me" at the end of every line, and surrounded by blue fire and piebald horses in the last scene. [It] is a part which is not to be sneezed at.

While the performance was going on, Mrs. Pelby was observed to be very restless and odd in her deportment, standing sometimes upon one leg, then balancing herself on the other, rubbing the upper ends of them together, thumping herself with her cocked hat in all sorts of places, and whispering such disjointed sentences as:

"I can't bear it!" "What shall I do?" "Good heaven! It's dreadful!" "I shall certainly go mad!" "I must pull them off!"

And bang would go the cocked hat against the skirts of her coat, both before and behind, with her fingers extended as if itching for the luxury of an uncontrollable scratch. During a pause, in a confidential manner and imploring accent, she said to Cowell (old Joe):

"Oh! I am in torture; for heaven's sake make an act at the end of this scene. That beast, Mrs. Tatnall, must have put cow-itch in my pantaloons!"

And so she had. "To what extreme may not a woman's vengeance lead!"

The Mount Pitt Circus was destroyed by fire in August, 1829. Previous to its destruction, a law had been passed requiring a license of $250 to be paid, and it in consequence was not at that time used for equestrian performances. It cost Sandford $100,000, and was mortgaged to Henry Yates, Esq. No insurance could be effected on it.

In 1832, I find a circus troupe traveling through the State of New York and known as Bancker's company. The following were some of the performers: J. W. Bancker, D. C. Callahan, Joe Blackburn, S. Blaisdell, Mons. Doer, H. Madigan, George Stone (clown), William Stone, and G. Plimpton, the celebrated Kent bugler. On the 9th of April they exhibited at Albany.

In May, 1832, the Boston Amphitheatre was opened under the management of W. & T. L. Stewart. In October, 1834, a temporary circus was erected on Mathewson Street, Providence. It was opened on the 14th.

A circus company performed in Sansom Street, Philadelphia, between Eighth and Ninth, in 1833. On the benefit night of the clown, George Stone, March 17th, 1834, the following persons volunteered: Messrs. George Blythe, Murphy, Wood, and E. Clark, the dwarf. The celebrated elephant, Ali Kahn from Calcutta, also appeared. George Blythe was the riding master.

Cooke's Circus arrived in this country in October, 1836: This troupe was second only to Astley's in Europe. It comprised from thirty to forty of the finest animals ever imported, some full blooded Arabian, and a number of most remarkable Burmese ponies, not much larger than Newfoundland dogs. Mr. Cooke had, in sons, daughters, and grandchildren, thirty-seven in his own family, nearly all of whom assisted in the performances. A new theatre was erected for him at the southeast corner of Ninth and Chestnut Streets, Philadelphia, and called Cooke's Circus. I present a copy of the opening bill:

COOKE'S EXTENSIVE EQUESTRIAN ESTABLISHMENT, AND NEW ARENA, CHESTNUT STREET, NEAR NINTH

will open on Monday, Aug. 28, 1837, and each evening during the week at 7 o'clock. Performance to commence precisely at ½ Past 7 o'clock. The whole of the entertainment will embrace an assemblage of talent and splendor not to he surpassed---the performances will be produced with the utmost grandeur and peculiarity of effect, embodying in the same evening the most unequalled scenes in the Circle, and Evolutions of Manly agility. Extraordinary horsemanship by Messrs. James Cooke and Woolford, Principal Equestrians, together with the full display of the abilities of the beautiful Stud of Horses and wonderful group of Burmese Ponies, with the performance of the infant Equestrian Prodigies, and a succession of novelties, which constitute one of the most varied, animated and interesting spectacles ever presented to an American public.

The performances will commence with a splendid Equestrian Cavalcade, entitled the Amazons and Warrior Chiefs---Master George Cooke's exercises on his little vaulting steed---Mr. Woolford and the

Persian steed, "Rege Pak," in an equestrian sketch, called the Omrah's Charger, or horse of 5,000---Mr. James Cooke's graceful horsemanship, representing the games Zephyr and Cupid---Novel Gymnasia by the Polish Brothers---Mr. Cooke's grandchildren will perform a new scene in the arena, entitled Gulliver and the Lilliputians---La Belle Rosiere on a fleet courser, by Mrs. Cole---at this period of the performance, an interval of fifteen minutes.

The Second Part will commence with Mr. Cooke's double leaping through various objects, and jumping over twelve horses---Mr. A. Cooke's light riding and leaping act---Mr. Wells will represent the Antipodean, or world upside down---The beautiful twin ponies, Hyder and Fatima, the greatest curiosities in America---Mr. Jas. Cooke will give a flying steed the Carnival of Venice. The entertainments will conclude with One Hundred Masquerades on Horseback.

Director of the Circle, Mr. Cooke, Junior.

Riding master, Mr. Woolford.

Clowns, Messrs. Williams and Wells.

The interior of the Circus will present a style of Elegant Decorations, combining the extreme of classical neatness and every variety of Magnificent Ornament. The Boxes embellished in a superior manner, with a distinct entrance to this elegant portion of the Circus. The Pit will be found spacious, and will command a distinct and full view of every part of the Circle. Saloons are attached to the Boxes and Pit, with every accommodation to render the visitors comfortable

The Decorations over the Circle will be of the most superb description, including a Splendid Ceiling, suspended from which a Massive Gold Candelabra, the largest in the world, emitting 2,500 lights, designed and executed by Mr. J. Foster, late principal Artist to the King's Theatre, the Italian Opera House, London. The Circus erected by Mr. Hopper, builder, from plans and drawings by Mr. Barlow, Architect to this establishment. The whole of the Gas Apparatus, Fittings, etc., by Messrs. Newton and Whelan. The orchestra will be efficient, and conducted by Mr. Sprake, Professor of Harmony, Clarionetist, etc.

Price of admission:---Boxes 75 cents; Pit 50 cents---children under 10 years of age, half price.

On the 17th of November the manager gave a benefit to the following institutions: Asylum for the Blind, the Widows' Asylum, and for the Disabled Firemen. The entire receipts were given without any deduction whatever. During the season the following novelties were announced for the first time: Mr. Cooke's horse, Sultan, would bring a kettle of water off the fire to his master; also take a fish out of the water, feats never attempted by any horse. The season closed December 21st and the company proceeded to Baltimore.

W. A. Delavan opened a circus at the corner of Front and Laurel Streets, Philadelphia, December 7th, 1836, for a short time. Frank Whittaker was equestrian manager; Rockwell, clown. The corps was composed of many of the most talented equestrians in the country and were accompanied by a stud of Arabian horses.

The season of 1838 at Cooke's Circus, Philadelphia, commenced March 12th. Among the company I find the following: Master G. Cooke, W. Cooke, A. Cooke, William and James Cooke, Mr. Cole, H. Cooke (*corde tendue*), Mr. Cooke Jr., ringmaster; Woolford, director; Williams, clown.

The season closed on the 26th of the same month with a benefit to Wm. and Jas. Cooke. On the 29th it was re-opened for one night only for the purpose of a complimentary benefit which was tendered to the manager. The price of tickets to all parts of the house was fixed at $1 each.

This building was a magnificent one. The diameter of the ring was 43 feet, offering a considerably larger space than was ordinarily allowed to equestrian performances. To this there were three entrances sufficiently spacious to admit of two horsemen riding abreast.

While playing in Baltimore at the Front Street Circus and on the morning of Saturday, February 3rd, 1838, the building was destroyed by fire. The decorations and properties of the circus company were entirely consumed, including his stud of nearly forty horses, twelve of which were remarkable for being extremely small. "Mazeppa" was the spectacle the night previous. Mr. Cooke had no insurance and his loss was total. Of fifty-two horses connected with this establishment, only five were rescued. Mr. Whitby, the head groom, had barely time to seize his clothes, which were hanging over his head in the stable; but had the presence of mind, though surrounded by smoke, to open the gate and let loose the horse Mazeppa. But he would not or could not get out.

The following letter from Mr. Thomas Hamblin to Mr. Cooke fully explains itself. It is one of the most honorable and creditable evidences of kind and generous feeling I have ever met with. It gives me pleasure to record it:

New York, February 10th, 1838

MY DEAR SIR: Amongst the numerous friends who sympathize with you in your sudden and extensive loss, I, whose personal experience teaches me to estimate it fully, am one who regrets it sincerely; at the same time my knowledge of your active disposition assures me that you will rather adopt measures immediately to repair the misfortune than lose time in idly lamenting it; and it gives me much pleasure to hear that committees are forming to aid you in the attempt. For my own part, having no theatre at command, my power to aid you is necessarily small, but if you will accept of my theatrical horse, Mazeppa, as a slight token of sympathy and regard, he is yours---with one condition only, that you never part with him to a stranger. He laid the first stone of a fortune, lost by a disaster similar to yours, and I should never have parted with him for the sake of "Auld Lang Syne" but for the hope that he may aid you in the same good service. Besides, my example may induce others who have circus horses, to present them, and thus the most serious (because the most difficult to supply) part of your loss will be repaired. Heartily wishing that this may be so, and giving you full power to use my name in any manner it can help you.

I am, dear sir, your friend,

Thos. S. Hamblin

On the 19th of February, Messrs. Fogg & Stickney, managers of the Amphitheatre at Cincinnati, gave Mr. Cooke a free benefit at their theatre. Messrs. Bates & Surtees, the proprietors of the theatre, gave the use of the building and all persons connected with the establishment volunteered their services.

Mr. Cooke then visited Philadelphia and leased the American Theatre (now Walnut) and opened it on Monday, April 2nd, 1838. I give his salutatory:

The public are respectfully informed that MR. COOKE will occupy for a short season the American Theatre, in Walnut Street, in order to present to the citizens of Philadelphia some equestrian and melodramatic spectacles, in a style hitherto unattempted for outlay, magnificence and effect.

A CARD, AND ESPECIAL NOTICE TO RESPECTABLE FAMILIES.

The utmost care and circumspection will be exercised in the admission of visitors to every part of the Theatre, in order to secure the confidence and comfort of such parents, guardians and husbands as may choose to visit this theatre during the run of performances advertised. In a word, every exhibition of immorality shall be peremptorily excluded, and to this arrangement MR. COOKE positively pledges himself to his friends and patrons. From the immense disbursements indispensable to the representation of stage and equestrian spectacles, in order to effect which, in the most complete style, the best available Talent of the period has been engaged. Mr. Cooke submits to public opinion, the necessity of raising the ordinary prices of the Walnut Street Theatre in a very trifling proportion, in order to meet his additional and extraordinary expenditure; therefore the Boxes will be 75 cts.; the Pit 37½ cts.; Gallery 25 cts.

For the first time here will be produced Lord Byron's beautiful dramatic tale of MAZEPPA and the Wild Horse. In which a most Powerful Double Company of Dramatic and Equestrian Performers and a New Stud of Beautiful American horses will appear and every incident of the Poem be realized. The piece arranged and produced under the entire direction of Mr. Woolford ---the new scenery by Mr. Russell Smith---the music composed and arranged by Mr. Sprake---Leader of the Orchestra, Mr. Jamieson, of the Bowery Theatre, New York---the Splendid Properties, Dresses and Decorations by Mr. Foster---the machinery, Platform, Bridges, etc., under the direction and superintendence of Mr. Barlow---the Beautiful Spotted horse Mazeppa, (one of Mr. Cooke's late purchases) trained for the Wild Steed by Mr. Whitby, head equerry to the establishment.

The Castelian of Laurenski, Mr. AMHERST (of the Theatre Royal, Drury Lane, London, his first appearance in Philadelphia); Rudzloff, Chamberlain of the Household, Mr. FOSTER (of the T. R. Adelphi, London); Olinska, daughter of the Castelian, Mrs. COLE (her first dramatic appearance); Abder Khan, King of Tartary, MR. RODNEY (from the Baltimore and Washington Theatres); Mazeppa, his son, under the name of Cassimer, Mr. WOOLFORD; Premislaus, Count Palatine, Mr. COOKE, Jr.; Drolinsko, Mr. GATES (of the late Bowery Theatre, N. Y.); Zemila, Mrs. HERRING (of the Bowery Theatre, N. Y.). For the numerous characters see bills of the day.

In the course of the spectacle will be vividly portrayed and acted to the life by Man and Steed, the following incidents, etc: The Court Yard of the Castle of Laurenski by night---Grand Nuptial Procession of the Palatine's Envoy on horse and foot---Nuptial Chariot drawn by Lilliputian Ponies---Ceremony of affiancing a Polish Bride---Grand Arena of the Castle---Surrounded by Galleries, Towers, Pavillions--Triumphant Car drawn by Six Beautiful horses---Charioteer, Mr. William Cooke---Ancient Tournament---Encounter of men at Arms---Carousal and Chivalric Sports, comprising Broad Sword Combats---Light play with the Small Sword---Contest of mounted Knights and crowning the Victors---Hall of Armory---Dormitory of the Castle---Desperate Conflict of Mazeppa and Count Palatine---Doom pronounced---Terrace of the Castle commanding an extensive view of the Mountainous Country, with precipices, cataracts, and bridges---Watch Tower and Beacons, in which this powerful description will be realized---The career of Mazeppa and the Wild horse, with all the horrible accompaniments of his flight, delineated by a moving panorama---Plains or Steppes of Tartary---with the precipitous mountains and the retreat of the Prophet Khan---Rural Sports and Songs of the Tartars---Shepherds calling their steeds---Awful Storm and fear of the Volpas---Arrival of Mazeppa on the exhausted and worn out steed, who sinks beneath his fatigue!---Interior of Tartar Tent, opening upon the grand encampment of the tribes---Mazeppa rescued from assassins and proclaimed King of Tartary---Review of the Tartar Forces and departure for the Invasion of Poland.

A Grand Pas de Trois.

Bridal Festival and Hymenal Ballet.

Terrible Conflict of Horse and Foot.

Grand Tableau.

Previous to the spectacle a popular farce.

The season closed May 5th, with "Mazeppa," after having enjoyed an unprecedented run.

V

In 1832, George Stone appeared at the Boston Circus as clown. Rockwell, D. C. Callahan, Johnson and Madigan were in the corps. The circus that for a time showed in Sansom Street, above Eighth, Philadelphia, in 1832, was on the lot now occupied by the stage and stables of the present Continental Circus.

In June, 1833, a circus and menagerie was erected in Southwark, Philadelphia, opposite Commissioner's Hall, South Second Street below Queen. Asten was the ringmaster; Buckley was the clown. In the troupe were Messrs. Jackson, Shay, Spencer, Eaton Stone, Andrews, J. Nathans, T. Nathans and De Camp. Andrews was the slack rope performer. The elephant, Tippo Sultan, was to be seen. He was imported by Capt. Skinner in the ship, Bengal, in 1819. He was the elephant that rescued J. Martin from the tigers that escaped from the cage while exhibiting in New York in 1826. This animal was ten feet high and had a pair of tusks four feet in length.

The Lion Theatre, Boston, on the site of the present Melodeon, was open for equestrian exhibitions and horse dramas in 1836, 1837 and 1838; and though the bills were excellent and well played, the experiment was eventually a failure. Here "El Hyder," "Mazeppa," "Timour the Tartar," "Rockwood," "The Forty Thieves," "The Cataract of the Ganges," and "The Secret Mine" were brought out and with immense success.

Cole & Co. 's Circus was exhibiting through the West and Southwest in 1837. In August they pitched their tent at Lexington. Among the company were S. B. Haven, Jackson, Whitlock, George Stone (clown); Turner, Stout and Whittaker; equestrian manager, A. Martin.

Yale, Sands & Co. were in Louisville, Ky., with a troupe of equestrians, January 25, 1838. George Stone, clown; Mr. Jackson, slack rope performer.

Messrs. Cole, Miller, Yale & Co. were in St. Louis in 1838 with an equestrian troupe. They were located at the corner of Second and Prune Streets. In the corps were R. Sands, equestrian manager; Howes, Jackson, E. Sands, Stokes, Eaton Stone, George Stone (clown); Turner, John May, N. Turner, Billy Whitlock, Master Smith, Alexander, and D. Stone.

In 1838, Joe Blackburn, clown, and Levi J. North, sailed for England. They opened at Astley's, London, in July. North appeared as the American champion, vaulting against Price, the champion of all Europe; having two springboards in the ring at once and two parties, American and English, with the colors of each country on the heads of their horses; Blackburn playing clown to the American party. I extract the following from a letter written home by Blackburn:

> You may well imagine my feeling (as well as North's) the first night; I must say I was frightened dreadfully; not for myself, but for North. I thought he would be so excited that he might get beat; but the trial came, and such a brilliant audience I never had the honor of making a bow to before; nearly two-thirds ladies; even the four or five front seats in the pit were filled entirely with ladies. Nearly all the foreign ambassadors were in front, also Taglioni, the great dancer. Great excitement prevailed. The time arrived, and Price threw only twenty somersaults. Then came the applause; they were certain North could not beat it, but the little Yankee went on and beat him scandalously, doing thirty-three. Such a shout I never heard—I thought the house would come down.

The English sportsmen in those days showed "fair play" to all and "let the best man win." They contended together twelve nights and North was beaten only once, which was on the 4th of July when Price beat North [by doing thirty-]five. The whole number thrown during the nights was for North, 414; Price, 357; majority for North, 57. The largest number thrown was by North on the eleventh night when he turned forty-one somersaults. The manager of the "show" was Ducrow; and the highest salary paid by him was for his best rider, £6 per week; and Price, the vaulter, received the same. A number of other performers got from £1 5s to £2. North and Blackburn received twelve guineas per week. On the occasion of North throwing his "forty-one," he was presented by Ducrow with a medal. On their return to this country they were very heartily received.

Messrs. Buckley, Hopkins & Co., with an equestrian corps, opened in Philadelphia, October 3rd, 1838, for two weeks at the corner of Filbert and Broad Streets.

Raymond and Waring opened Cooke's Circus, Philadelphia, November 25th, 1839, with a troupe of equestrians, together with a stud of Arabian and Appaloosas horses; also the elephant, Pizarro, and two Arabian pack camels. Howard, Dale, McCollum, Buckley and Minnich were in the corps. Lowry and Williams, clowns; equestrian director, Joe Blackburn. Mons.

Le Fort, the French rider, and Otto Motley, appeared during the season.

Rufus Welch opened the Walnut Street Circus (now Continental), Philadelphia, November 22nd, 1841, for a season of forty nights. The company was composed of the following: Amherst, William O'Dale, John Glenroy, Jennings, William Spencer, Sig. Ivan Showeriskey, Miller, Mestayer, and Young McCollum. The equestrian director was Cadwallader; ringmaster, Jennings; Yankee clown, Rockwell; Mezzo clown, Wells. During the season the following persons put in an appearance: Buckley, T. V. Turner and Joe Sweeney. Season closed February 26th, 1842, with a benefit to Riley and Son. [They] re-opened March 30th, with W. Mulligan, John Glenroy, Miller, Mestayer, G. Sweet and Mrs. Louisa Howard. Mr. Levi North appeared on the opening night in a full transformation act, entitled "Italy, France and Spain." He was announced as just arrived, crowned with honors, from the courts of Europe. The season lasted only ten nights.

Cooke's Circus, Philadelphia, was opened as the Olympic, September 30, 1842, for a short season. Master Diamond appeared in his Negro eccentricities.

Welch opened the Walnut Street Circus as the Olympic, March 18, 1843. In the corps were Hernandez, Ruggles, Master Billy Kincade, Conover, Cadwallader and Hobbs.

In 1843 the Walnut Street Theatre, Philadelphia, was opened for equestrian performances. I append the opening bill:

CIRCUS AT THE WALNUT STREET THEATRE.

The manager having made arrangements for a limited period with Mr. N. HOWES, the director of the celebrated EQUESTRIAN TROUPE, whose recent unrivaled performances in New York, Boston, etc., at the principal theatres, have elicited so much applause from FASHIONABLE AND OVERFLOWING audiences, respectfully announces that the FIRST GRAND EXHIBITION, at the above establishment, will take place on SATURDAY EVENING, Nov. 4th. The following well established and talented performers are engaged:

Equestrian Director, Mr. Needham.

Ring Master, H.C. Johnson.

Clown, D. Gardner

Mr.T.V. Turner,	Mrs. Gardner,
Mr.George Sweet,	Mrs. Cole,

Mr.W. Howes,	Mrs. Sweet,
Mr. McFarland,	Mrs. Perry,
Mr. Perry,	Mrs. Johnson,
Mr. Johnson,	Mrs. McFarland,
Mr. Lebrun,	Mrs. Rodgers,
Mr. D. Gardner,	Master Aymar,
Mr. Jno. Reed,	and
Master Vincent,	La Petite Amazone.

Prices of admission---boxes, 50 cents; second tier, 25 cents; pit, 12½ cents. Doors open at 6½ o'clock. Performance to commence at 7.

Part 1. GRAND POLISH CAVALCADE, By twelve Knights and Ladies. The beautiful pony, FANNY ELSSLER, will be introduced in a variety of feats. Master Alexander Vincent, in a most brilliant act of horsemanship. Grand display of ground tumbling by the troupe. Nautical act of horsemanship by T.V. Turner. Duet, by Mr. and Mrs. Gardner. Mr. Perry will appear as the Comanche Chief.

Intermission of ten minutes.

Part. 2. Mr. G. Sweet on the tight rope. Leaping and somersetting by the Voltiguers, led by McFARLAND, the hero of 60 successive somersaults. Mrs. Gardner in the act of Lady Sylphide. Comic song by Dan Gardner. Herculean feats of strength by Mons. Lebrun. Transformation act by G. Sweet.

Part 3. The beautiful pantomimic scene of Cupid and Zephyr, or the Sprites of the Silver Shower. Gymnastics by Mr. Gardner and Master Vincent. Act of horsemanship by T.V. Turner. To conclude with the pantomimic sketch, called COL. TILTON.

In a short time John Kay was added to the company as clown. In February dramatic performances were given in conjunction with the ring performances. Barney Williams was in the company and between the performances would tell an Irish story, sing a song and dance. Occasionally he would play a small part in the afterpiece. The season closed August 26th, 1845.

The National, Philadelphia, was soon after opened by the same company. In the corps was Miss Louisa Howard (now Mrs. Frank Brower), Frank Rivers, and Master Richard Rivers. Mr. James Bancker and his horse, Emperor, were among the features of the performances. Frank Pastor, Sig. Germani, Nathans, Levi North, T. V. Turner, Mme. Mario, Mme. Carter, McFarland, and

Wm. Kincade were added during the season. A full dramatic company was also engaged and "Mazeppa" and "The Cataract of the Ganges" were produced in excellent style. Season closed April 11, 1846, with a benefit to W. A. Delavan.

Welch, Mann & Delavan, previous to their departure for the West, opened in Philadelphia at the National, Ninth and Chestnut (for two nights), May 4, 1846. Frank Brower was engaged and delighted the audience with a collection of his Negro eccentricities.

This theatre was opened by Welch & Mann in 1846. I subjoin the announcement:

CIRCUS AND NATIONAL THEATRE.

The public of Philadelphia are very respectfully informed that on MONDAY, OCTOBER 5th, the Circus and National Theatre will be opened for the Winter Season, under the management of Messrs. WELCH & MANN, in a style which they flatter themselves must ensure a continuance of that distinguished and fashionable support which has invariably attended this very popular resort since it has fallen under their uncontrolled direction.

The whole of the Interior has been rendered singularly elegant by a rich classic light and novel style of Decoration, in which the most gorgeous effects that burnished gold can produce will be chastely heightened by a ground of cream color and pure white.

The Splendid Chandelier (an exhibition in itself) will emit numberless Gas Lights, casting upon the Stage, arena, and indeed the remotest part of the edifice, a light as cheerful and brilliant as the sun at noon-day.

The Furniture is entirely new; the fabrics of the seats and of the reposes are of the best quality; the mats and carpets are of the most brilliant patterns, all purchased in this city.

The doors will be opened at 7¼ o'clock---to commence at a quarter before 8 o'clock.

On entering this extensive equestrian temple, the spectator will be gratified with a splendid Drop Scene, the work of the whole summer, and founded on the memorable description of Lord Byron's Dream, painted by that universally esteemed artist, John Wiser.

The Prices of Admission will be: First Tier and Parquette, 25 cents; To the Second Tier, 12½ cents; Colored Gallery, 12½ cents; Colored Boxes, 25 cents; Seats in Private Boxes, 50 cents; Whole Box, $6.00.

Notice to the Public---In order to prevent any disappointment, the patrons of this establishment are advised to purchase tickets and secure places for the evening, which can be done without any additional cost, by application at the Box Office, from 9 o'clock in the morning until 3 in the evening.

The visitors and patrons of this most fashionable arena will be welcomed and saluted by a full Orchestra of great talent, led by the very celebrated Mr. St. Luke, of Palmo's Italian Opera House, who will commence with and direct the National Anthem; and in the course of the evening introduce the favorite airs and pieces of the most admired French, German and Italian Operas.

The following brilliant program of the scenes, acts, tableaux and cavalcades, is submitted to the public for MONDAY EVENING, Oct. 5th, as a series of novelties will be given on Wednesday, and on the following evening. The opening pageant and grand pas de course will be rode and maneuvered by a joint company of principal male and female artists, entitled THE UNION OF CHIVALRY AND BEAUTY, Most Magnificently Appointed.

Pas Eccoisais, Par la Petite, Mary Anne Wells. Followed by the most splendid and finished equestrian act ever presented within the walls of any arena, by the superiorly gifted and graceful Master Richard Rivers, who will exert himself to sustain the high degree of favor with which he was received last season. A Local Ditty, by Mr. Robinson, the very popular comedian, his first appearance in this city. An exhibition melee of Arena Gymnastics, by a troupe of unequaled talent. Succeeded by an Equestrian Extravaganza, entitled Le Festin de Polichinel, or Equestrian Masquerade, rode in various characters of metamorphosis by Master Chambers, his first appearance before the public of Philadelphia. Grand pas de Danse, by Miss Louisa Wells, pupil of the celebrated Madam Hazard. The terrific and heroic act of the Undaunted Saracen, or the Cry of Liberty! by the celebrated Mr. Walter Howard, the great Southern scene rider. The very diverting and wonderful act of the Enchanted Ladder, by Master R. Rivers. The first part will close with that admirable exhibition of Equestrianism, which has already enchanted thousands, and which will now be presented here, under the title of America's Daughter, or a Woman's honorable effort in her Native Land, in which, after a long and severe indisposition, Mrs. Louisa Howard will have the honor of re-appearing before her numerous friends and the public of Philadelphia, on her fine steed, Maximilian.

An intermission of 10 minutes will be given.

The Second Part will commence with a noble and extraordinary display on the Floating Cord, in order to introduce that very esteemed and elegant acrobat, Wm. Day. A very droll ditty by Mr. Robinson. Followed by the renowned West Indian rider, Mr. Glenroy, Jr., pupil of Mr. Cadwallader, who left this city two years since, with every promise of a high reputation and unbounded success, and after the acquirement of innumerable laurels, returns to the friends of his youth, in his Professional Act! on a single horse, without saddle or bridle, introducing his somersets, leaps, etc. More will not be said, as his friends, the Philadelphians, never forget those Artistes who aim to secure their good opinion by persevering industry. He submits himself to their judgment. The unequaled classic poses of the Three Brothers Rivers. To conclude with the amusing and everywhere popular extravaganza of THE HUNTED TAILOR, or, Off to the Election.

Equestrian Director, Mr. Cadwallader. Ringmaster, Mr. N. Johnson. First Clown by the celebrated Dan Rice, a Mimic and Buffo of the first and highest reputation, his first appearance here. Second Clown, John Wells.

John Gossin was afterwards added to the corps as clown. On the 31st of November, Sands and Lent made their appearance. Lathrop and Pentland were also engaged as clowns. Il Sig. Germani appeared in his East Indian Jugglerie, riding backwards. Mr. Sands introduced his ponies, Deaf Burke and Tom Spring; also his dancing horse, Mayfly. Master Hernandez appeared on the 7th of December. On the 12th, Jesse and Maurice Sands took a benefit. Master Aymar appeared during the season; also Mr. Kemp, who performed his feat of running on a barrel. William Marchael and son appeared in their posturing acts. Frank Whittaker appeared in a French extravaganza. January, 1847, Marie Macarte appeared in a splendid act. [The] season closed May 8, 1847, with a benefit to Dan Rice.

[They] re-opened October 18, 1847, for the winter season: riding master, F. Whittaker; clown, John May; manager, Joseph Foster. On the opening night, Prof. Kirby, the great American acrobat, and his children appeared. Mrs. Louisa Howard appeared December 15th in a mythological single act, called "The Meeting of Flora and Minerva." E. Derious, J. J. Nathans and T. Mosley appeared. Season closed April 22nd, 1848, with a benefit to the manager.

[It] re-opened under Foster's management, October 23rd, 1848: Horace Nichols, ringmaster; John May, clown; Hercules S. Lee gave his cannon ball exercise; Lavater Lee, E. C. Lee, W. Walker and La Petite Sequi Lee were the acrobats; W. Walker, corde volante; Mrs. Louisa Howard was the principal equestrienne. Mary Ann Wells, Sam Lathrop (clown), and Washington Chambers appeared during the season. On the occasion of the benefit of Miss Mary Wells, Jim Sanford appeared and gave a Negro song and dance. [The] season closed March 17, 1849.

[It] re-opened as R. Sands & Co.'s Hippoferaean Arena and American Circus for a short season.

Monday evening, October 22d, the Performance will commence with a superb Cavalcade; Comic song, Dickerson; Master Jesse Sands in his daring feat of equitation; Deaf Burk and Tom Spring, the fighting ponies; W.H. Stout and Ben Stevens, as the Slaves of Greece; Cinderella and Black Diamond; Feats of Magic and Globe Performances; Messrs. Stout and Aymar, in the feat entitled the Revolving Spheres; Henry Gardner, as Mazaroni, the Brigand; Scenes in the Desert, in which the Camels and Arabs will appear; the Fete of Jove; Mr. George Sergeant in a classic performance; May Fly, the English Dancing Horse; Master Maurice Sands in a beautiful act. To conclude with a Comic Pantomime.

Clowns---Joe Pentland, John May and Frank Brower.

Master of the Arena---Capt. J.A. Decamp.

Equestrian Director---Mr. W.H. Stout.

Leader of the Orchestra---Mr. E.K. Eaton.

Madame Armand, the most celebrated foreign equestrienne in the world and late of the Tacon Theatre, Havana, appeared November 26, in "Le Pas de l'Echaipe." December 10th, Dan Rice appeared as the Shakespearean clown; also Frank Rosston, the favorite ringmaster, and Master Jean. W. F. Wallett, the English clown, and Joe Pentland, the clown of America, appeared December 17th. [The] season closed January 5th, 1850, with a benefit to Wallett.

[It] re-opened November 5th, 1850, Rufus Welch proprietor, when was presented: the "Scourge of the Desert," Master Derious on the "Enchanted Ladder," principal act by Master Rivers, vaulting by the corps, "Frolics of Flora" by Mlle. Eloise, comic song by E. Dickinson, six horse act by Mr. Stickney, Mr. Rivers and sons as the Olympic Posturers, "Circassian Lovers" by Camilla Gardner and W. O. Dale, Mr. Stickney's horse Cincinnatus, cannon ball scene [by] Herr Lee, bar act [by] Eaton Stone, and concluded with the Ethiopian extravaganza of "High Life in Philadelphia, or Jenny Lind at Home."

VI

The Robinson and Eldred Equestrian Company, composed of Mme. Louisa Brower, Master James Robinson, Lavater Lee and family, and Hernandez, were on a Southern tour in 1850. In November they were at Columbia, S.C., and gave the net proceeds to the Orphan Asylum of that place. Frank Brower was the clown.

In February, 1851, Welch, McCollum and Risley took a company of equestrians to England and opened at Drury Lane Theatre, London. In the corps were Mlle. Caroline Leyo, Mme. Louisa Brower, Mr. McCollum, Eaton Stone, Mons. Louisset, Young Baptiste, etc., etc. Mme. Brower (formerly Louisa Howard) was very highly spoken of by the press of that city.

In 1851 the National Circus, Ninth and Chestnut Streets, Philadelphia, was opened for equestrian performances. Eaton Stone, Sam Lathrop, Mlle. Eloise, Thomas Neville, the Rivers Family, and W. F. Wallett were in the corps. For the benefit of S. V. W. Post, leader of the orchestra, the New Orleans Opera and Ballet Troupe appeared.

[NOTE.---In answer to a correspondent from New Bedford, requiring information in regard to Francis Ricketts, the writer of these articles would say that in 1798 Ricketts lived at No. 52 North Street, Sixth Ward, Philadelphia. This is the last time I can find his name in the City Directory. He sailed for England with his brother and was never after heard of. The vessel was lost. The only property he left behind him was a portrait of old John B. Ricketts and said to be very fine. It was sold at auction about eight years ago and was purchased by Peter Grain, a Philadelphia gentleman. Although it was purchased for a mere nothing, yet I understand that so highly does he prize it that money cannot purchase it.]

At the National Circus, Philadelphia, March 17, 1851, a Complimentary Benefit was tendered Lewis B. Lent. Eaton Stone, Miss Randolph (first appeared in the circle), Hill, Lee, Mlle. Eloise, Rivers Family, E. Derious, Richards, and Mrs. Camilla Gardner appeared. The season closed this night.

On the first of May, this establishment was opened by Gen. Rufus Welch for four nights with the French Troupe. Lathrop, clown; F. Whittaker, ringmaster; S.P. Stickney, T.

Neville, Mons. Benoit, J. Miller, Lee, Richards and Master James Smith were in the corps.

[It] re-opened November 3, 1851; Rufus Welch, proprietor; L. B. Lent, director; J. M. Nixon, equestrian director; Messrs. Worrell and Whittaker, clowns. The program was as follows: musical comicalities, by Edam Dickinson; Miss Sallie Stickney as the Queen of May; the ponies, Romeo and Juliet, in their wonder-inspiring feats; Mr. Neville in his terrific feats on horseback; "*Les Freres d'Olympie*," by Messrs. Benoit and Richards; *Pas Seul*, Miss Wells; Mlle. Marie in her *Scene d'Equitatio;* battoute leaps by the gymnastic corps; four horse act by S. P. Stickney; Mr. J. M. Nixon and his children in their act of classic gymnastics; juggling on horseback by Mons. Benoit; the trick horse, Cincinnatus, introduced by Mr. S. P. Stickney; dashing barrier act by Mr. D. Richards; feats with real cannon balls by Herr Lee.

Mlle. Louise Tourniaire, the French equestrienne, appeared on the 20th of November. Joe Pentland joined the forces on the 24th of November, 1851. On the 9th of March, 1852, the season closed with a complimentary benefit to Levi J. North. The performance consisted of Levi J. North and Mlle. Marie in the pleasing double act of horsemanship, entitled the "Shepherd and Shepherdess." Mr. North introduced his infant daughter, only five years of age, in an act of equitation. Mr. North introduced his pupil, Mr. Willie, in his performance, entitled the "Hurdle Race." Mr. North appeared in an equestrian scene, entitled the "Sprites of the Silver Shower." Mr. North exhibited his horse, Tammany, which executed seven different dances. Mlle. Tourniaire appeared in her Grand Scene Equestre. On the 15th of March, John May appeared as clown. [The] season closed May 4th with a benefit to Rufus Welch.

[It] re-opened November 1, 1852, by Rufus Welch, with ring and dramatic performances: W. F. Wallett, clown; Mlle. Miona, equestrienne. During the season, Le Jeune Burte, D. W. Stone, W. W. Nichols and Mlle. Rosa appeared. [The] season closed March 24, 1853, with a benefit to J. Myers.

On the 1st of December, 1853, the Walnut Street Circus, Philadelphia, was opened as Raymond's Zoological Institute: S. P. Stickney, equestrian director; Jim Myers, clown; B. Kipp, treasurer. In the course of each exhibition, Prof. Langworthy entered the den of his lions, leopards, cougars, tigers, etc. The equestrian performances embraced the following wonderful and brilliant scenes and acts in the circle: grand full dress entree; antipodean feats on the Polandric ladder; acts of juvenile horsemanship, etc., etc., etc. [The] season closed January 28, 1854.

[It] re-opened as [the] Philadelphia Circus, November 1, 1854, by Messrs. Welch and Lent. Among the most prominent members of the company were Miss Sallie Stickney and Mlle. Marie, the accomplished equestrienne; Mr. H. W. Franklin, T. Neville (first appearance since his return from California), J. M. Nixon, S. P. Stickney, W. Kincade, J. Hankins, W. Odell, F. Whittaker, T. King, W. Franklin, B. Stevens, W. Laine, H. Nagle, Master Luke Rivers, Robert Stickney, George Nixon, W. Nixon, Misses Sophie and Irene Worrell, etc; Billy Worrell, clown. Mr. Robinson, the comic vocalist, made his first appearance in Philadelphia on the opening night. During the season, Le Jeune Burte and his father appeared. April 21, 1855, Dan Rice, with his horse, Excelsior, and the comic mules, appeared. [The] season closed April 24 with a benefit to Dan Rice.

[It was] re-opened by Welch & Lent, November 12th, 1855: S. E. Harris (right name Wesley Barmore), stage manager; J. G. Cadwallader, equestrian director; F. Whittaker, riding master; W. Worrell, clown. Ring and stage performances were given. A star ballet troupe [was] headed by Mlle. Zoe and Mons. Wiethoff. Among the company were Mlle. Zoe, Mlle. Henry, Miss Waldgrave, Rose C. Henry, Kirby, W. A. Wood, Virginia Sherwood, Mlle. Marie, H. Magilton, H. W. Franklin, T. Neville, the Motley Bros., C. Sherwood, W. Franklin, G. Dunbar, F. Donaldson, H. Worland, J. E. Johnson, F. Whittaker, J. Rivers, J. R. Hankins, H. Bertine, and Bill Worrell, clown. March 13, 1856, Dan Rice appeared with his horse, Excelsior, and "them" mules; also the Fellanti Family and Mons. De Bach. [The] season closed in March.

[It was] re-opened by L. B. Lent, October 20th, 1856, with a full dramatic and equestrian corps. [The] season closed April 11th, 1857.

May 22nd, 1857, Franconi's Colossal French Hippodrome, from Madison Square, New York, opened in Philadelphia on the lot on Broad Street near the Baltimore depot.

Welch's National Circus, Eighth and Walnut Streets, Philadelphia, opened by Dan Rice's Great Show, February 18th, 1858. During the season he introduced his trick animals, viz.: rhinoceros, tight rope elephant, waltzing camel, low comedy mules, and talking horse, Excelsior. The whole was under the immediate control and supervision of the American humorist, Dan Rice. On the 31st of March, Mr. James Melville, the great Australian bareback rider, appeared for the benefit of Dan. [The] season closed April 5th with a benefit to Melville.

[It was] re-opened by L. B. Lent, November 8th, 1858. Dr. James L. Thayer, Sam Long and Dan Gardner were clowns. In the equestrian corps were H. Magilton, F. H. Rosston, William Kincade, Sallie Stickney, Ella Laroux, Camilla Gardner, Jennie Johnson, Mary Ann Cole, Mme. De Bache, and Mlle. Elsie, the child rider.

On the 21st of April, 1859, VanAmburgh's Zoological and Equestrian Troupe showed in Philadelphia on the lot on Spruce Street, between Tenth and Eleventh Streets, preparatory to starting on their summer tour. They exhibited here only three days and then left for the western part of the state. In the company were the Madigan Family, Dr. James L. Thayer (clown), Nat Austin, Carpenter, Kincade, Norton, Armstrong, etc., etc.

Dan Rice, with his Great Show, opened Welch's Circus, Philadelphia, for the season, October 31st, 1859. On the 22nd of March, 1860, Tony Pastor, the celebrated clown, appeared. The second season closed March 31st. The season was a very prosperous one and Dan gained considerable notoriety by his great speech to the students of that city during the excitement among the John Brownites.

Nixon & Co.'s Circus, known under this specific heading, dates from the commencement of January, 1849. For a considerable time prior to that, an organization had been traveling as Nixon & Kemp's Circus and had also performed in New York several weeks in the fall and early winter of 1858. The company, as first designated, was intended for a season at Niblo's Garden, where it began operations on the 27th of January, 1859, with an efficient corps of performers, including Melville, bareback rider; Mme. Moran, equestrienne; Dan Costello, clown, and "Don Juan," the educated Bull. During its stay at Niblo's, which extended to the 9th of April, this troupe experienced a large share of patronage; for which, it must be confessed, a strong endeavor had been made in the purchase of Dan Rice's share of the stock known under his name, at the cost, it was alleged, of $25,000. While at Niblo's, too, several novelties in the spectacular style were brought out; Dan Rice also making his appearance. From time to time the troupe received various additions, including Madames Tourniaire and Josephine, equestriennes; Mlle. Ellsler, tight rope dancer; Nat Austin, necromantic horseman and clown, and others.

In April, 1859, prior to taking a more extended tour, the troupe visited in succession: Hempstead, Jamaica, Flushing, Williamsburgh and Greenpoint, on both the Long Island and Jersey sides. In the following month it was in Providence, R.I., whence it proceeded to Massachusetts. Mons. Gregoire, the "strongest man in the world," joined the company about this time and went with it to New Hampshire and Canada East, whence it proceeded to Connecticut, terminating the season at Springfield, September 1.

On the 31st of October the troupe made a public entry into New York and immediately commenced business in a spacious tent at the junction of Thirteenth Street and Broadway. Mr. J. M. Nixon became sole lessee and left for Europe with Mr. Moore, stage manager at Niblo's Garden, in search of novelty wherewith to inaugurate the winter season at the above establishment. Concurrently, the National Theatre (Chatham) was opened as a circus under the ostensible lessee-ship of Messrs. W. T. Aymar and L. Nixon, which induced the belief that Mr. J. M. Nixon was the responsible party; but that gentleman's connection with the concern was formally denied and therefore no longer credited, Mr. J. W. Tryon being considered as the lessee.

The company at the National, which included Tony Pastor, Tom Neville, W. Aymar, Louisa Wells and several other clever performers, continued to hold together for a few weeks.

While abroad, Messrs. Nixon and Moore came to arrangements with several performers, among whom were certain members of the Cooke Family, long and widely known as equestrians. With these and a stud of horses they opened at Niblo's Garden on the 16th of January, 1860. Foremost among the performers on this occasion were the Hanlon Brothers, acrobats; Mlle. Ella Zoyara, equestrienne; Robinson, bareback rider; Joe Pentland, "court jester;" W. Cooke, who did numerous things *a la* Rarey; and several other very clever persons.

At first the company did not give the satisfaction anticipated. This was jointly attributable to getting matters in working order too soon and to the discovery that but few of the celebrated company, announced to have been well drafted from, had really been engaged. This objection, however, was withdrawn when subsequent representations proved that the troupe, made up of English and American professionals, was a highly meritorious one. It remained at Niblo's from January 16 to March 3, inclusive; leaving for Boston, where it commenced on the 5th and remained till the return to Niblo's, recommencing business there on the 9th of April. It continued as above until the 26th of May, when the company, with some changes, went on a tour embracing Philadelphia, Baltimore, and several other places. On July the 30th, we find it once more at Niblo's where its final performance was given on the 14th of September. Subsequently, it visited Washington, Richmond, Norfolk and Portsmouth, Macon, Ga., [and] on to New Orleans and ultimately Havana, where it commenced a season the last week in December and where it yet remains.

VII

Rufus Welch was born in New Berlin, Chenango Valley, N.Y., September, 1800. He was bound an apprentice to a cabinetmaker but did not serve out his time. At nineteen years of age he joined a circus troupe and became soon afterward a member of the firm of Purdy & Macomber as a partner and advertiser. They were well known throughout the country and did a thriving business.

About 1828, Stickney & Fogg erected a very neat circus building on the Old York Road, Philadelphia, which was called the Washington Amphitheatre. At that time, Welch was forming a circus troupe for the West Indies and offered Levi J. North an engagement to join his corps for that destination. North had just completed his apprenticeship with Fogg. Charles La Forest also was engaged and, with these promising young riders, Welch made a successful tour. He returned to the United States, still pursuing his locomotive equestrian performances. His partners soon after changed their business and, relinquishing circus affairs, collected one of the most imposing menagerie exhibitions that this country ever saw, which realized to the proprietors vast sums of money. They opened about 1830 in Maeizel's Hall in Fifth Street, near Prune, Philadelphia, and returned to that locality during several winters following.

Whilst they were exhibiting there, a vessel from the East Indies, having on board the celebrated elephant, Caroline, entered the Delaware and ran aground on a shoal and was likely to become a total wreck. The animal was consigned to Purdy, Welch & Macomber and the insurance companies, despairing of getting the animal out alive, were disposed to abandon the risk. Gen. Welch rigged a derrick with slings and succeeded in hoisting the animal out. A well trained and faithful dog was thrown overboard as a pioneer, who swam towards the nearest shore. The elephant followed and both animals got safely to land.

Gen. Welch soon after sailed for Africa for fresh animals. Landing at the Cape of Good Hope, he penetrated nearly two thousand miles into the interior of the country in company with some English gentlemen who had a taste for lion hunting. In this trip he secured several splendid lions, tigers, elephants, and two large giraffes, and succeeded in bringing the entire invoice, which cost $64,000, safely to Boston. The firm continued in the menagerie business for some years. They sold out to a company called the "Zoological Institute."

Gen. Welch then joined in partnership with Alvah V. Mann and the firm opened a circus in Broadway, New York, opposite Niblo's Garden. This was a temporary affair under canvas. Shortly after this they visited Philadelphia. Raymond had erected a circus building in Walnut Street, near Eighth, and had failed there. Welch, Mann & Delavan became the managers and gave winter exhibitions. In summer, this company was divided---Delavan, Nathans & Co. took the northern circuit, whilst Mann & Bancker attended to the middle and other states. Of these circuits I shall speak hereafter.

After the failure of Burton at the National, Philadelphia (originally Cooke's Circus), Gen. Welch took a lease of the house for a term of years and rented it out in summer and other vacations when not used by himself for theatrical performances. In 1844, Wemyss & Oxley failed there and Welch & Mann established an amphitheatre on the extensive scale of Astley's in London. About 1851, Gen. Welch, in company with Levi J. North, the boy Hernandez, and others, proceeded to England and opened the American Circus at Drury Lane Theatre. Subsequently, he traveled through France and Germany.

In 1853, Mons. Franconi came to the United States and established the Hippodrome at Madison Square, New York. This establishment was conducted in a style of novelty unknown in equestrian performances. It was a vast amphitheatre, having no stage but enclosing a stadium over which were run chariot races and upon which other exciting displays were made. The novelty of this exhibition attracted vast audiences and Gen. Welch, stimulated by national pride, determined to excel it. He prepared an immense pavilion tent, engaged daring riders, and conducted "The American Hippodrome" on a scale of magnificence hitherto unparalleled. Immense crowds were attracted but the cost of the exhibition was tremendous and the business did not pay. Welch's hippodrome was taken as far as New Orleans, where the company was dissolved, the management having sustained a very heavy loss. Returning to Philadelphia, the general entered into partnership with Lewis B. Lent. The firm met with a sudden check to their prosperity by the burning of the National Theatre and Circus, corner of Ninth and Chestnut Streets, during the performance of "Raymond and Agnes." In the autumn of 1854, Lent & Welch opened the Walnut Street Circus, which they called the National, now known as the Continental. It was during the management of this establishment that Gen. Welch died, which occurred December 5, 1856. His disease was typhoid fever. He had traveled in almost every country in the habitable globe. He crossed the Atlantic fourteen times and has probably journeyed as far, and perhaps farther, than any man now living. During his varied career, he lost and made several fortunes. His generosity of character and charitable disposition were proverbial. He always had an open hand for the distressed and none knew him but to love him. He lost more by his own liberality than by reverses in business. He was universally esteemed by members of the profession and there are few of them now living who have not been indebted to him for advice, counsel, protection and assistance.

> I shall not look upon his like again.
> He was a man, take him for all in all,
> He should have died hereafter.

John Grimaldi Wells—right name John Willis—clown, died at Philadelphia in 1852. An inoffensive man and clever fellow, he was himself his only enemy.

Joe Claveau, clown with Howes & Mabie's Circus, committed suicide in Iowa City. He was a good fellow. He had visited, professionally and often, most of the West Indies Islands, many portions of South America, Mexico, etc., and in 1836-37 was a member of the Ravel Family.

Joe Buckley, equestrian, died at New Albany, Ind., of cholera in 1843.

John Aymar, a performer of great merit, was killed by a fall in England in 1814.

William F. Stone died at Nevada, Cal., in the fortieth year of his age. He was extensively known as an equestrian performer of great ability and as a man of many good and charitable qualities. He was brother of George Stone, the celebrated clown. He traveled many years in company with Foley.

John Weaver—a Herculean performer—died of bilious fever at Fort Meigs, Ala., with Bancker's Company in 1831. He was a Philadelphian. The clergyman presented a bill for divine service.

Mr. [Alexander] Downie died at the West Indies while with Welch's company. He was a most accomplished equestrian.

J. H. Amherst, well known as connected with Gen. Welch's Circus, died in Philadelphia in 1851 at an advanced age.

Fred Golson, the celebrated clown and pantomimist, died in New Orleans.

Lewis B. Lent, circus manager, [was] born in Jamestown, N.Y.

Moses J. Lipman, [was] born in South Street, Philadelphia.

Levi J. North, born in Brooklyn, N.Y., in 1813, [was] married in England to Miss Sophia West, youngest daughter of James West, formerly proprietor of the Walnut Street Circus.

[Col. Hugh] Lindsay, "Old Hontz," the clown, through his connection with the show business, acquired a widespread popularity and acquaintance and in his days, by his inborn natural talent and wit, probably contributed as much to the hilarity, mirth and amusement of mankind as any man living. He was born in Philadelphia in April, 1804. At the age of fifteen years he engaged himself as an apprentice to the show business with J. E. Myers and Lewis Mestayer, who kept a sort of show room in Market Street, above Fourth in Philadelphia, consisting of gymnastic performances, wire walking, jugglery, etc. Subsequently, he became connected with the traveling circus and menagerie of John Miller (the pioneer of the business) of Allentown. While with Miller he attended to the door, acted clown, and drove the camels. Subsequently, he engaged with Weyman's traveling company. This was in 1823-4. After this, he re-engaged with Miller's company, then under the management of Rufus Welch. In 1825, Mr. Miller sold out his menagerie to Mr. Crosby of New York for $4,000 and Lindsay engaged under the new proprietor. Of the company, John Miller was a great wire performer and Dan Minnich the best activity performer in the United States at that time; so they had a team in full. They performed through the spring and summer over parts of Pennsylvania, Maryland, Virginia, New Jersey and Delaware, in a great many cities, boroughs, villages and at country inns. In the winter of 1825-6, Lindsay performed at the Pennsylvania Museum at Eighth and Market Streets in Philadelphia. About this time he became acquainted at the Black Bear Hotel in Third Street with a young lady from Lehigh County, named Lydia Panley, which finally resulted in marriage in 1828. After this, he engaged with the traveling companies of Messrs. Fields & Ponier, Aaron Turner, H. Hawley, and Mills & Harrison.

In 1831, Lindsay and Mr. Nathan Miller bought up a lot of horses and broke them for the ring, got a new canvas and engaged a company of equestrian performers. In Allentown they gave their first exhibitions. They then started on a tour through the country and arriving at Norristown, Pa., Mr. Lindsay sold out his interest in the concern to a Mr. Buckley, an English clown.

The same season, Mr. Miller also sold out and, returning to Allentown, commenced the study of law. He still resides among us, is hale and hearty, and in the full enjoyment of the comforts of life. His father, Mr. John Miller, accumulated by his exhibitions about $60,000.

In 1832, Lindsay set up in the business for himself on a small scale and shortly after brought before the public as a pupil, S. S. Sanford, a son of his sister, now one of the most popular Negro delineators in the United States and the proprietor of Sanford's Opera House in Philadelphia. Among his other pupils in the show business are Stout, Nagle and Shindel, the equestrians. He continued in the business until within a few years ago, when he went to tavern keeping in Northumberland County; and about a year ago moved to Berks County, the place where he brought his eventful career to a close, as above stated.

In 1844 the Whigs conceived the brilliant idea of getting Lindsay to stump the lower German counties, holding out hopes of remunerating him with a fat office. The colonel did his work but whether effectually or not we are not prepared to say, as the counties to which his humorous efforts were confined gave increased Democratic majorities. His political life gave him distaste for the show business and it was some time before "Old Hontz" again enlivened the country folks by his presence. As soon as the Whigs secured a majority in the House of Representatives, Lindsay came on and applied for the office of Sergeant-at-Arms; but failing to get it, he became disgusted with politics and carried "Old Hontz" out to the country again. In 1848, the Whigs tried to get him on the stump again to play the buffoon but Lindsay was not to be caught a second time. "Take Lindsay for all in all, we shall ne'er look upon his like again." He was a warm-hearted and generous man, having probably disbursed in his day, for the benefit of others, a hundred thousand dollars, and at last died comparatively a poor man. He was about fifty-six years of age.

Colonel Alvah Mann, formerly connected with Gen. Welch as manager, died in New York, July 9, 1855. The colonel had his faults and some good qualifications. He was buried from the Florence Hotel. His last speculation as a manager was in the circus, corner of Sixth Avenue and Thirty-Ninth Street, New York, in 1852-3, which was unsuccessful. He was a native of New York State.

Lafayette Circus, New York, situated in Laurens Street, near Thompson, Leonard and Canal Streets, [was] opened by W. Sandford in 1825.

Richmond Hill Theatre, New York, was transformed into an amphitheatre and opened October, 1833, with a good equestrian company.

Bowery Amphitheatre, New York, was remodeled in 1837 and occupied by June, Titus, Angevine & Co. In 1851, it was opened for one season by S. B. Howes' company. Subsequently, the circus troupe of Sands, Nathan & Co. performed in the building up to the termination of the twenty years' lease in 1853.

The first circus that ever visited Albany, N.Y., performed on the open lot near Old Fort Orange. The riders were Mr. and Mrs. Stewart from England. They had no canvas, nothing but stakes and ropes forming a ring for the riders. Collections were taken up by the clown among the audience outside the ring. Mrs. Stewart was a fearless, graceful rider.

VIII

Ricketts' English Circus, after being burnt out at the corner of Sixth and Chestnut Streets, Philadelphia, 1795, proceeded North, performing in New York and Albany....

West's company performed in Albany in 1820 in the "Old Colonie," now Broadway, back of a stonecutter's yard. His company performed several seasons at the Broadway Circus. They first produced "Timour the Tartar," "The Cataract of the Ganges," "Blue Beard," etc. West, after selling out to Price & Simpson of the Park Theatre, New York, returned to England wealthy.

The palmy days of Price & Simpson's Circus began to decline in 1826. One beautiful animal was saved of the entire stud, "Fanny Mare," that was lost in the gale from Baltimore to Charleston. It was described as a heart-rending scene. The poor animals followed in the wake of the vessel until they disappeared, one after another, beneath the waves. After this disaster, circuses seemed to have died out.

There was a circus on the hill in Albany, just above the old jail in State Street, corner of Eagle Street. Parsons was the proprietor. This was before he opened the Pearl Street show in 1824. It was on this spot that Joe Martin exhibited his wild beasts. Tippo Sultan, the great elephant, was the star, being the second elephant ever seen in America.

Tippo saved Joe's life in the Bowery, New York, in 1822, under the following circumstances: Two tigers had got loose from their cages in the absence of the keepers. Martin came into the caravan at this moment. One of the tigers had torn the llama to pieces and was feeding on it. The other tiger had attacked the lion, the lion holding the tiger in "chancery." The tiger that was feeding upon the llama then made at Joe, who had a cane in his hand and kept him at bay till he got to the elephant, who, quick as thought, with his trunk placed Joe in safety on his back. Tippo threw the tiger with great violence to the roof of the building. The alarm was given and the animals secured. It was a most miraculous escape for Joe.

This circus consisted of John Stickney and wife; Bill Gates, clown [and] many years low comedian at the Bowery Theatre; Jim Westervelt, rider (died from the effects of a fall from his horse at Syracuse); Mat De Garmo, son of Dr. De Garmo of Albany; Jake Burton, an Albany boy (Poor Jake died in the mines of Galena.); Ned Carter, slack rope.

The wonderful pony, Billy, thirty inches high, was a great curiosity in those days. Old Bill Jones was the groomsman of this circus, and I believe is still living in Albany. There was also a theatrical entertainment given here. Duffy played "Timour," the stage being "mother earth." The dressing rooms were in the rear of the old jail. Mrs. Thompson played Zorilda. Her charger flew up the steps like a cat. She sang comic songs and danced the slack wire. She was alive a few years ago, the wife of an actor named Chip. Mrs. Pritchard, formerly Mrs. Tatnall, played here. She married Sam Hosick, the son of the celebrated Dr. Hosick of New York.

I have a letter in my possession from Mrs. P. She was then in New Orleans. She says: "I am now about to leave New Orleans forever," etc., etc., and she did. The steamboat which she was on, took fire on [the] Red River and she perished. She was a beautiful woman but not an excellent actress. Her performances were showy, fustian, [and] perhaps an agreeable rant. [She was] a brunette with expressive black eyes, flowing black hair, Grecian nose, and a small mouth, set off with splendid pearly teeth. Having been bred to dancing, she was very graceful in action. While living with her husband, Mr. Pemberton, in the West Indies, she became acquainted with Sam Tatnall, the equestrian, and he, representing the vast field that was open to her talents in the United States, made love to and eloped with her to the States, where she opened at the Broadway Circus, New York, as an equestrienne. She then visited Philadelphia and opened at the Walnut Street Circus, September 4, 1824, and made quite a hit. [She] opened December 22nd at the Chestnut [Street Theatre] as Florinda in "The Apostate" but the result proved that she did not possess the legitimate claims to Thalia. As Little Pickle, in "The Spoiled Child," she was excellent.

Blanchard's Circus visited Albany in 1826 and joined Parsons at the North Pearl Street. This company had been playing at Quebec. Blanchard was an Englishman. He died at Louisville, Ky., in 1837 and was buried by the Masonic fraternity. His son George is living in this city. Cecelia Blanchard broke her leg while riding at Utica, 1828, and it had to be amputated. William, the bareback rider, died in Martinique, W.I., 1831. Blanchard opened the new Amphitheatre, Baltimore, in 1820 and realized a fortune but subsequently lost all. He opened the old Chatham Garden, New York, as a circus and failed. For many years he kept a small inn on the Bloomingdale Road. Mme. Blanchard is now a French cook in New York. Cecelia is still living in New York.

The immortal "Nosey Phillips of "Free Lunch" memory was Blanchard's right-hand bottlewasher at this time. I hear "Nosey" is defunct. Well, if he is dead, he has paid one debt at all events. So peace to his gags!

There was a show shop at the corner of Division and Green Streets, Albany. Circuses, etc., flourished here for a short time in 1823-24. Old Vilalave and family danced on the rope here.

The Amphitheatre of Parsons in North Pearl Street, Albany, where the Methodist Church now stands, was probably one of the most spacious and perfect in all its appointments in the Union. The ring and stage were immense. The rear of the building was constructed with an opening into a garden over a hundred feet in depth, thus affording a grand display in getting up such spectacles as "The Cataract of the Ganges," "Blue Beard," "The Siege of Montgaiz," etc., with processions of men, horses and elephants, producing a grand and truly imposing effect. The following are the names of the equestrian corps: West (ringmaster), Master Jake Burton, Rockwell, W. and James Bancker, Callahan, Bill Gates (clown, afterwards first low comedian at the Bowery Theatre, New York), Mrs. Williams (equestrienne), Hunter (the greatest bareback rider in the world), Stickney, etc. The dramatic company consisted of: Kenyon, Thompson, Lamb, Laidly, Stevenson, Henry Eberle, Somerville, C. W. Taylor (now "Old Charley Taylor" but then a young man with flowing ambrosial locks), Logan (father of Eliza), Avery, Roper, Mrs. Hatch, Mrs. John Cooke, Miss Eberle, Miss Hatch, Mrs. Lamb, Miss Robertson, etc. "The Cataract of the Ganges" and spectacles of the like character were brought out here in a style of splendor probably never before equaled. The stud of horses were not surpassed in number, splendor or dexterity. The celebrated horse, White Surry, was one of the most graceful, beautiful, learned creatures that ever entered the ring. Surry did the "leading business" in "tricks," storming fortresses, dashing up cataracts, and other wonderful feats.

Henry Rockwell, a beautiful boy from Utica, was one of Parsons' apprentices at the old North Pearl Street Circus. He was manager of various companies of the United States. He erected a theatre in Cincinnati and at one time was quite wealthy. He failed in business and died shortly afterwards. A gentleman by the name of Bagely, of Albany, was his guardian. His life was strange and romantic. It never was rightly known who his parents were.

I will relate an incident that occurred some twenty-five years ago which may be interesting. I was standing in company with Rockwell one cold night on the corner of Camp and Poydras Streets, New Orleans, in the fall of 1830. An English woman approached us with two small boys, about five and seven years of age. She seemed weighed down with grief. She asked if we knew of any humane person who would take her children and rear them. She had married a second husband, who was a Balize pilot, and she resided with him at the Southwest Pass of the Mississippi River. This spot is one of the most dreary, God-forsaken places I ever saw, the pilots' houses being erected on piles and surrounded by swamps, drift logs, alligators, etc. The poor mother informed us that her husband had formed an ill feeling toward her children and she had come up to the city at his request to get rid of them or never return herself. Rockwell took the oldest boy and a man by the name of Outlaw, a constable, took the other. It was a heart-rending scene to see the mother and children part forever! Outlaw, being a man of dissolute habits, neglected the child that was given him. It died soon afterwards, I learned, of yellow fever. Rockwell trained the other little fellow in the arts and mysteries of the ring and he soon became a great favorite.

The company commenced its tour through Florida and Alabama. "Little John," that was the youthful rider's name, was taken sick. The physician pronounced it a hopeless case. The company was obliged to leave for other towns northward; so we were reluctantly compelled to leave him---and, as we supposed, forever---in the hands of strangers. Many years passed and the fate of "Little John" remained a mystery.

I happened to be in New Orleans on another occasion and one night at a masquerade ball a rough, sea-faring man approached me and asked my name and if I knew one Rockwell. He was the step-father of John C. He informed me that his wife had been dead many years. Before she died she had received a letter from her son in Alabama. This was "Little John." He recovered from his sickness and, like Oliver Twist, had fallen into the hands of a good Samaritan. He married his benefactor's daughter. Now the curtain drops on this strange drama. The youthful rider I have spoken of was one of the filibustering party, under Lopez, who was captured and garroted at Cuba a few years ago.

[Andrew] Ducrow was a famous rope dancer and rider. He was the proprietor of the great Astley's Amphitheatre in London. Both Ducrow and Astley were exceedingly ignorant. They were, however, *au fait* in their profession. Old Astley (an Englishman) used to talk of a "krocker-dile wot stopped Hellexhander's harmy hon the Halps, hand ven 'e vas cut hopen 'e 'ad han hindividual hin full harmor hin his hinards."

Ducrow was a wonderful man in his way. He first produced the great spectacle of "Mazeppa." It was written for his theatre by a Mr. Milner and took all London by storm. The original person that played the part of Mazeppa at Ducrow's is now living in Philadelphia. His name is John Cartlitch. He was handsomely provided for in the will of Ducrow. Mr. Cartlitch at present keeps a cozy little ale house in Fourth Street, below Vine, Philadelphia. He is quite aged, but fat, jolly, and has plenty of the world's "rocks."

Herr Andre Cline, the celebrated tight rope dancer, at a rehearsal in Ducrow's establishment, declined ascending on a tight rope from the stage to the gallery, deeming it a dangerous experiment. Ducrow said:

"What, sir, afraid? I am not afraid and am not afraid of hurting myself. Give me the pole."

And in dressing gown and slippers, Ducrow ascended and descended. The performers shuddered at the feat.

Herr Cline was born in London. His brother, Andrew, a Herculean performer, was born in Germany. Thomas, another brother, was a melodramatic actor of the old Franklin Theatre, New York. His daughter is Jerry Merrifield's wife. Thomas S. Cline's first appearance in America was October 7th, 1835, at the Chestnut Street Theatre, Philadelphia, as William in "Black Eyed Susan." Francis Cline was leader of the orchestra for many years at the Chestnut, Philadelphia.

Herr Cline made his first appearance on the American stage at the Bowery Theatre, New York, in 1828. [He] first appeared in Philadelphia November 2, 1828, where his graceful movements on the elastic cord astonished everyone. Having accumulated quite a fortune in England, he brought it to this country and deposited in the United States Bank, which failed and he was a ruined man. He lost $40,000. His father, a German, was living in Philadelphia a few years ago.

The celebrated Ravel Family came to this country during the cholera of 1832 (July). They then consisted of ten performers: Jean, his wife and little daughter; Dominique (the oldest child of Mme. Lanati, a widow, whom Gabriel married in Boston'); Gabriel, Antoine and Jerome; Miss Emily Paque, whom Jean Ravel married some years later; Louis Marzetti, then only nine years of age; and Jean Pebernard, a favorite prodigy, afterwards disabled by an accident to his foot and now a shoemaker in Cincinnati.

They made their first appearance at the Park Theatre during the same month of their arrival in this country and first appeared in Philadelphia September 13 of the same year. Their performances consisted of rope dancing, Herculean feats, and pantomimic ballets in four parts, in which the Young Gabriel sustained the principal characters. They then made a tour South and West and in 1834 returned to Europe, where they divided into two troupes: Jean Ravel, Dominique and Marzetti traveling in Italy and Spain and the three brothers proceeded to London, where they appeared January 5, 1836, at Drury Lane. On the 7th of September, 1836, they started for New York, where they played from October, 1836, till July, 1837. In New Orleans they remained a long time.

They lost all their baggage and properties by the snagging of a steamboat on the Mississippi. Returning to New York, they set sail for France. [After remaining] at Toulouse for six months, in 1842 [they] again set sail for New York and opened at Niblo's. In a short time, Gabriel, Jerome and Antoine left for home. Francois remained behind and with the troupe visited Cuba, South America, Brazil, Chili and Peru, returning to the States in 1846. At the destruction of Niblo's Theatre, September, 1846, they lost $5,000. On the 20th of January, 1847, Master Javelli, brother of Leon Javelli, died in New Orleans of consumption. In October, 1847, the four brothers started for home. Marzetti remained and joined the Lehmann family. In 1848, Francois returned, bringing the Martinetti family with him. In 1849, Antoine and Jerome returned to America. Paul Brilliant, Josephine Bertin and the Lehmanns were now in the troupe. Gabriel remained at Toulouse but in 1851 he came over and joined the company.

Yrca Matthias, the danseuse, joined the Ravels in 1853, making her debut October 31 at Niblo's. She first appeared in Philadelphia January 9, 1854, at the Walnut in the ballet of "Piquita." She soon after married Francois Ravel. On the 20th of November, 1857, she sailed for England.

In 1858, Marietta Zanfretta, one of the greatest female tight rope dancers in the world, was engaged with this company. Zanfretta is very young, only twenty-three, and very pretty, with those black, lustrous Italian eyes that pierce like an arrow. Her form is exquisitely symmetrical and while the exercises of her specialty have strengthened her muscles they have not impaired her grace. Her movements are as lithe as those of a panther. She never uses the balance pole but poises herself on the rope without any advantageous aid. She performs the same feats on the *corde tendue,* which I think surprising in a dancer on the firm floor. She runs backwards and forwards, turning with incredible rapidity, dances on the rope, stands on the point of one toe, descends the angle of the rope into the parquet, and re-ascends unfaltering and fearless. Indeed, her doings are unexampled. Zanfretta is a Venetian by birth. Her parents pursued the same line and her earliest steps were on the rope. She debuted in this country at Niblo's and created the greatest enthusiasm by her performances.

Mons. Blondin, a Frenchman by birth, whose right name is Emile Gravelet, was engaged in France in 1855 by the agent of William Niblo to perform with the Ravels at Niblo's Garden, New York. He made his first appearance in the fall of that year. He continued with this troupe for a number of years; then he went with the Martinetti family. For two years he was connected with a circus company as part proprietor. He married a lady of this country and built a magnificent place at Niagara, the cost of which exceeded $5,000. He is the most graceful and daring performer on the tight rope in the world. Those who have seen him perform will remember the ease and precision, as well as the extraordinary grace with which he accomplishes his feats. On the 30th of June, 1859, he accomplished the wonderful feat of crossing the Niagara River on a tight rope, carrying a man on his back, at a height of one hundred and fifty-one feet above the rushing torrent below, an exhibition which stands without a parallel. The rope was three and a quarter inches in diameter, 1,300 feet long and, including the guy ropes, cost $290. It was made in two sections and was spliced by a sailor. About 12,000 people witnessed the crossing by the intrepid performer. Since this feat he has accomplished many others far more daring.

During the past three months he has appeared at the different theatres throughout the country in his wonderful exercises, among which are the following: the wooden shoe dance; dancing on stilts fastened to the logs; thrilling chair feat, sitting, standing and dancing upon the chair whilst resting on the rope; backward somersaults, foot to foot over burning candles, a terrific feat; the violin feat, turning back somersaults while playing a favorite air; astounding drum feat, throwing a somersault while beating a drum; terrific cataract ascension from the back of the stage to the farthest limit of upper gallery of the auditorium, during which he executed many of the more daring feats performed by him over the boiling chasm of Niagara, crossing the rope blindfolded and enveloped in a sack, standing on his head, throwing a back somersault, and concluding by walking the whole length of his narrow footing bearing on his back any one of the audience who might desire to accompany him. During Mons. Blondin's late engagement in Baltimore, the writer of these articles accomplished the feat of going and returning on Blondin's back, one hundred feet above the audience, and landed in safety.

Blondin's last engagement in this country (previous to a single night at Niblo's, January 14, 1860) was at the Troy Museum, N.Y. He soon after visited Niagara and, disposing of his estate at a great sacrifice, is about to sail for Europe with his wife and children, having made up his mind not to visit America again. Blondin is about forty-three years of age.

There has been a great deal said by the press about Blondin, when, if it was known, there are several French and Italian rope walkers on the other side of the Atlantic who can perform the same feats that Blondin does. We have in our very midst two excellent performers, Mons. De Lave and Richard Hemmings. In many things Mr. Hemmings is really excellent and his performances on the wire last season in this city were the wonder and astonishment of all and stamped him a great performer. The first sight of his performance creates an uneasy sensation of extreme danger but his perfect aplomb and self-possession soon banish that feeling and your anxiety is lost in admiration of the wonderful display. Undoubtedly the extraordinary skill of Mr. Hemmings is owed partly to his coming from a race of rope dancers, for aptitude for particular exercises is unquestionably transmissible and it is very possible to be "to the manner born."

Mr. Hemmings is one of the best equestrians at present in America. He is a sort of Caleb Quotem, sometimes appearing in the ring as a gymnastic clown, at other times he may be seen as an equestrian, making extraordinary leaps, throwing somersaults. Other feats peculiar to himself---classic postures, leaping, jumping, somersaults, and other specimens of equestrianism---are all done in an easy and graceful style.

Ducrow produced one of the most gorgeous show pieces ever witnessed in London, "St. George and the Dragon." It was produced at the Drury Lane Theatre and replenished the coffers of the manager, Mr. Bunn, to the great joy of sundry and numerous creditors. The spectacle had an unprecedented run for many weeks. A beautiful testimonial was presented to Ducrow, consisting of a massive silver vase, for the admirable manner in which he had produced the spectacle.

Ducrow was mercurial in his habits, fidgety and cross-grained, especially when engaged in rehearsals. He would find fault with the accommodations for his horses. At Drury Lane, Manager Bunn refused to reserve a certain part of the house for his favorite horse. The piece was to be produced that night. Ducrow sent for Mr. Milner and requested him to read the articles of agreement between the parties for the production of "St. George and the Dragon" for so many nights, at such an amount, etceteras. To the surprise of Bunn, Ducrow had agreed to produce the piece but had not agreed to play in it himself. It was impossible to produce the piece without Ducrow as St. George, the hero of it.

"Now," says Ducrow, "tell the mummers (theatricals) hif they pay me £25 per night hextra for my hacting St. George, and allow my prads (horses) to 'ave comfortable quarters, hit's a go." The manager wilted and came to Ducrow's terms.

Mons. Gouffe, the man-monkey, was in one of Ducrow's productions. His right name was Goff and the bills of the day metamorphosed him into a Frenchman. He was a London cockney and he came as near imitating the monkey as any human being could, on or off the stage. He was brought to this country by John Fletcher, the originator of the Venetian statues and the celebrated pantomimist, in 1831 and made his first appearance November 29 at the Tremont Theatre, Boston, in the pantomime entertainment of "Jack Robinson." [He] first appeared in New York at the Bowery Theatre December 13 in "The Island Ape." [He] appeared in the same character at the Walnut, Philadelphia, January 2, 1832.

This extraordinarily gifted man exhibited one of the most accurate pictures of the peculiarities of the ape I have ever yet witnessed, the wonderful flexibilities of limbs, the perfect acquaintance with the most trifling habits of that animal, beggars the imagination; and the pathetic scene of his dying in the entertainment of "The Brazilian Ape" stamped him a man of most acute genius and observation. It would seem that either from natural conformation or from a high degree of practical discipline, he had acquired such powers over his limbs and could throw himself into such positions, as could appertain to no human being furnished with but an ordinary quota of joints and tendons. The muscular strength manifested by an individual of such dimensions was in itself a matter of great astonishment.

Mons. Gouffe had a wife, who made her first appearance in this country January 24, 1832, at the Camp Street Theatre, New Orleans, as Mysa in "Jacko."

IX

Astley's Amphitheatre, London, was first opened by a Mr. Davis as a circus. It was built in the first place by placing immense wagon wheels in the form of an amphitheatre (oblong). These were entrenched in the ground several feet. Large ship spars were then inserted in the hubs and packed tight with earth. This formed the foundation. It was covered and became a large amphitheatre. It went through many transmogrifications and, during Ducrow's management, it was burned to the ground in 1839. The loss was very great. Ducrow died shortly afterwards.

Astley's has existed for nearly a century. It has been rebuilt. Grimaldi flourished at Astley's. Grimaldi was in his zenith in 1811-12. I saw a recent account of his death a year ago. This must be a mistake. I ascertained when in England in 1835 that Grimaldi was then dead. He had a son then living. Dickens' *Life of Grimaldi* gives many interesting accounts of that wonderful man. He performed at three different theatres on the same night in London....

The great spectacle of "The Battle of Waterloo" was played at Vauxhall Garden and at Astley's and was from the pen of John Amherst, Esq. This piece was played at the Old North Pearl Street Circus, Albany. It was said the military equipment were the same that were worn at the real battle of Waterloo, purchased by the manager of Vauxhall Gardens from the British Government.

Amherst came to the United States with Cooke's Circus, which was burnt out at Baltimore in 1836. He was a fine classic scholar and a member of the English Dramatic Authors' Society of London. He was the author of many standard plays. He died at Blockley Hospital, Philadelphia, a few years ago. Edmund Connor, the actor, with true philanthropy, had the remains of Amherst brought from Blockley and buried from his own dwelling in Race Street. He was afflicted with various diseases, which rendered his existence almost insupportable to himself; and, conscious of their incurability, he, in a letter to the Actors' Order, after thanking the members for the kindness of which he had been a recipient, requested to be sent back to the almshouse, from which place he had been taken by the Order a short time before his death. His request was complied with. The Order, not yet "weary of well-doing," appropriated a further sum to supply him with books and writing material. Thus it will be seen that he did not die neglected or forsaken. His death occurred August 12th, 1851, and the expenses of his funeral were borne by the Actors' Order of Friendship.

Thirty-five years ago a sort of menagerie opened in the stable opposite Bowlsby's Hotel in North Market Street (now Broadway), southwest corner of Van Tromp Street, Albany. The lower part of the building is now occupied as a stove store, etc., and the upper by several families. Bowlsby's was considered a first class hotel in those days, equal to Skinner's and Rockwell's, afterwards called the City Hotel and Mansion House, the sites of those two celebrated hotels now being occupied by those magnificent structures, Marble Hall and Ransom's Building. Members of the Legislature and other dignitaries sojourned at this house. Members of the Legislature, be it remembered, in those days were high minded, honorable men, above bribery and corruption and free from the baleful influences of those land sharks, known as lobby members.

But to the show. It consisted of two cub bears; Dandy Jack, a gloomy looking monkey was the star; a calf with two heads; and a monster that was thrown upon the beach at Staten Island---at least so the showman informed the audience. [The latter] was drawn on four wheels and was about twenty feet long. It was a sort of "What Is It?" Its tail resembled that of a whale, its body was black and smooth, the head square, with a pair of eyes resembling two bungholes in a large-sized hogshead. Dr. Latham was the manager.

This menagerie was destroyed by a mob at Waterloo, in the western part of the state of New York. The manager had changed the "critter" to a whale---"very like a whale." The show folks besmeared it through the day with a very rancid kind of oil, the odor having the effect to keep the "meddling" audience at a respectable distance, as close examination would be fatal to the whale stock. A prying, meddlesome lawyer---a Yankee, of course ---felt extremely anxious to ascertain the exact thickness of the whale's hide. He accordingly took out his jackknife, regardless of the whaley smell, and cut a large hole in the side of the monster. The lawyer was completely dumfounded. The monster of the deep had a body made of sole leather! His tail was the only thing that was Simon pure about his whaleship. The manager and his assistants carried their wardrobes, trunks, etc., in the whale's belly---probably taking the idea from old Jonah! The head of the whale was portable, or "come-off-able." Suffice it to say, as soon as the trick was discovered, the mob "harpooned" the entire show. This was some time previous to Barnum's day and the art of humbugging had not arrived at such a pitch of perfection as that distinguished "showman" has since carried it. In fact, humbugging is now elevated to a pedestal among the fine arts.

At Parron Circus was a man by the name of Richardson, a horse breaker who sometimes officiated as the riding master.

Richardson had the management of a circus in Cincinnati some thirty years ago in Captain Woodruff's Amphitheatre on Sycamore Street. This was during an exciting political season. Two candidates for office, a lawyer and a doctor, had met on one or two occasions and had a shooting and stabbing match in public. The doctor was a wide-awake man and so he determined to rig himself with a coat of mail, consisting of a sheet iron breast plate, which he wore under his vest. His opponent was a "cutting man." Both of these fire eaters met in the boxes of the circus and at it they went. The doctor fired all his ammunition without, fortunately, damaging anyone. The lawyer used his knife on the ribs of the doctor without effect. Finally, they clinched and both tumbled headlong into the ring, the audience looking on, some with evident indication of horror and others with delight. The horses had just been brought into the ring. The groom made himself scarce, leaving the gladiators in possession of the arena. The fight was renewed with great fury, the lawyer cutting at some substance harder than the ribs. During the fight no person had interfered. Richardson was sent for. He rushed into the ring just as the lawyer was about to give the doctor his last dose. He seized Law and Physic by the collar and held them at arms' length and made a speech that never will be forgotten. Richardson was from Danbury, Conn.

John Gossin joined Bancker's company in Little York, Upper Canada. John was a native of Pittsburgh, Pa. He had been performing with an itinerant circus owned by one Bernard, a Yankee, who made a fortune and retired. Gossin performed the clown in an admirable manner and became an immense favorite throughout the United States. He married a beautiful woman at Lexington, Ky. She was the belle of the arena. Gossin was a fine looking man. He lived fast, commanded a large salary, partook largely of the fatal draught that "steals away the brain." He was finally divorced from his wife. She subsequently married a rich Spaniard of Havana. Gossin then became very dissipated, his spirits broken, his nervous system sadly deranged; and while in this maddened state committed a murder in the South. Gossin's brother was killed in a fracas on the Mississippi River by a gambler. Gossin then armed himself, met the murderer of his brother, and killed him on the spot! But he was acquitted and died soon after of yellow fever at Natchez.

John Gossin was with Sam Nichols' company that performed in the amphitheatre in Dallius Street, Albany. Gossin and "Jack" May both performed in this company and were a "whole team" as clowns. Nichols had a superb equestrian and theatrical company and for two seasons in succession did an immense business, the establishment being patronized by first class people.

The last time Forrest appeared in Albany was at the Nichols' Amphitheatre, then under the management, I think, of Jackson---familiarly known as "Black Jack." Josephine Clifton, the "Majestic Josephine," as she was called, played an engagement with Forrest at the same time.

In this company was also a person by the name of Vail. He was the successor of Weaver in feats of strength. He was a powerful man and a native of Mansfield, Ohio. His early days were occupied as a boatman on the Western rivers. Vail had many hairbreadth escapes from death. He performed his feats of strength on a pole that supported the large pavilion. It was crowded one night in a town in Indiana. Vail was suspended by his knees to the pole, which was some ten feet from the ground. In his hands he held two anvils and by his teeth he held several fifty-six pound weights. At this moment one of those fearful tornadoes, that we so often hear of in the West, suddenly came up. The pavilion was blown to atoms. The seats fell with a fearful crash. The howling of the wind and the screams of the women and children were terrible. The pole on which Vail was suspended was broken and he fell, with the great weights of iron he was grappling, head foremost to the ground. A number of persons were killed. Vail was picked up for dead among the mass of weights. He was badly injured but survived his fearful fall.

Vail had a fortunate escape from death during an earthquake at Martinique in the West Indies. The sides of the house that he occupied fell outwards. Vail was just in the act of leaping from the windows. He fell safely to the street, the window frame passing over his head and shoulders. So close was he to the falling beams that his foot became entangled in the falling mass and drew his leg from the boot as, he said, with a "patent boot-jack."

After this occurrence he was shipwrecked. He abandoned the profession and became very wealthy at Port Royal, one of the West India Islands. He married a quadroon, as rich as Croesus and as "lovely as a June flower." He is now located at Yankee Station, California, and is known as "Squire Vail, Justice of the Peace."

Young D. C. Callahan also amused the Albanians with his elegant and superb horsemanship. He was a native of New York. Most of his days were passed in Mexico and South America. He died in his native city, New York.

Joe Blackburn also performed on the Beaver Street lot, Albany. Blackburn was **the** clown of the American arena. He was a man of extraordinary ability. He possessed a good education and figured as a poet of no ordinary pretensions. His letters from Europe were perused with much interest and were published in the New York *Spirit of the Times* and other journals of the day.... His uncle left Joe his entire fortune but, poor fellow, whilst on his way from New Orleans to Baltimore to inherit his wealth, he sickened and died on board the steamer Express Mail near Horseshoe Bend, February 26, 1841, and was buried at Memphis, Tenn. His death was regretted by all who had the pleasure of his acquaintance. Many are the anecdotes recorded of him. *Requiescat in pace.*

One of the Memphis papers speaks of the procession to the grave of Blackburn in the following language:

The respective companies met according to previous notice, for the purpose of paying that respect due to the worth and talents of the late Joseph Blackburn. The procession then formed in front of the Commercial Hotel, Messrs. Garson and Claveau taking the lead. Then followed the New Orleans band, drawn in a car by six horses, followed by the New York band, drawn by six horses. The rear was brought up by the performers, citizens, etc., on horseback, bearing the usual badge of mourning on the left arm. The procession then proceeded to the burial ground, where it formed in a circle around the grave of the deceased; the bands played a dirge suited to the occasion; each member took the badge from his arm and placed it as a tribute of respect upon the grave of their departed friend. Mr. Garson and Mr. Herbert made neat and appropriate addresses on the occasion, after which the procession returned to the city.

The old North Pearl Street Amphitheatre, Albany, began to "gin in," or give up the ghost, about the year 1828. "Nosey" Phillips tried his hand in this place as well as at the South Pearl Street Theatre. Like all other projects that Nosey undertook, somebody was the sufferer. Nosey was as mad a wag as we shall never look upon his like again. His style of "financiering" were plans only peculiar to himself. He was the sole author and inventor of many shrewd and curious dodges. Moses---that was his Christian name---opened a theatre in Providence, R.I. He procured an excellent company from New York and with the aid of Providence he pocketed quite a sum. He owed several small scores to the inhabitants as well as actors. Nosey promised that all bills against him should be liquidated on Monday without fail. The bills of the day were issued and the lamps all trimmed, the actors "all up in their parts," and sundry creditors awaited the important moment; but the eagle-eyed, as well as eagle-**nosed** Nosey, had fled to New York with all the "rocks" in his fob! Arriving in that city, he had no difficulty in finding an old sufferer that he owed a long-standing bill. Nosey brought his wits to working order, knowing that in a few hours he would he seized for debt and be placed in durance vile. (There was a law for imprisonment for debt in those days.) He induced said old sufferer to sue him, which he did. Nosey acknowledged the count and was committed to jail. The enraged creditors from Rhode Island arrived only to be disappointed. Nosey was already caged for debt and in a few days all excitement had subsided. Nosey settled the score with his lucky friend and once more he "buckled on his armor" for fresh adventures.

Cincinnati was the scene of many of Nosey's jokes. Here he enlivened the audience of Fogg & Stickney's Circus by enacting the clown in a time-worn scene called the "Peasant's Frolic." Nosey was astride a beautiful black horse, telling some stereotyped "Joe Millers," when all of a sudden the horse flew round the ring as if a skyrocket was fast to his tail. The ringmaster could not stop him. Nosey's lungs were brought into requisition. He appealed to the man with the whip at the top of his voice:

"Stop him, for God sake!"

"A good joke," says the ringmaster.

"Go it, Nosey!" yelled the boys.

Nosey went it loose, heels over head, into the pit, striking an honest Jack Tar in the eye with his hand. Nosey's skull-cap and a small portion of his cap were missing. The sailor was enraged to find his eye blackened.

"Well," says Jack, "that feller with a big handle on his mug is the d--est wust clown I ever did see."

Nosey left the ring as soon as possible, as his tights had come down. A lawsuit was the result but the ringmaster declared it was a joke and, besides that, he could not stop the horse. Nosey was accordingly non-suited.

The next exploit was at Louisville, Ky., where Nosey advertised in glowing colors that he would give a grand masquerade ball, the dresses and masks to be furnished by the manager; and at the close of the masquerade several comic songs were to be sung, in imitation of old Jack Barnes, by the indefatigable manager. The night came, and the music, then the array of dancers. The crowd now began to inquire for the costumer---dominoes were in great demand and so was Nosey. But the bird had flown and was safely stowed away in the Hoosier state of Indiana.

Nosey modestly and very discreetly declined a second visit to this part of Kentucky---feathers and tar advanced in price as soon as the dodge was discovered. Many, **very** many of these innocent pranks Nosey engaged in. His grand wind-up, however, took place in New Orleans in 1842. Caldwell, manager of the St. Charles Theatre, dispatched an agent to New York with full power to engage the best talent to be found and in particular to engage Aaron Phillips---who was a good actor and worthy man---for his prompter. (Aaron Phillips was at one time the manager of the Chestnut Street Theatre, Philadelphia). Caldwell's agent, being a stranger in the capacity of theatrical negotiator, committed a sad mistake. He wrote a note, directing the same to Mr. Phillips, comedian. Nosey's hawk eye discovered the letter and received the contents with unspeakable joy, but "mum" was the word. He certainly was Mr. Phillips, comedian, and was a prompter.

The agent never was instructed to engage any other person for prompter but Mr. Phillips, hence the mistake. Nosey was placed under binding articles of agreement, which he signed. The other party agreed to give said Phillips the sum of $30 per week and a benefit at the expiration of six months. What was the surprise of Caldwell, the actors, and everybody, when the immortal Nosey arrived in New Orleans! Caldwell was in for it. Nosey was sent to Mobile but he got all the agreement called for. Here he officiated as prompter. Here he set his wormwood ideas. His prompting caused a bickering among the entire company.

Two of the actors, B. D. and Tom R., hit upon the following ingenious plan to have some amusement at Nosey's expense. It required great caution or a lawsuit would be the result. Old "Phil," as Nosey was sometimes called, went on the stage one night in place of some person who was ill. The only dressing room for him was with D. and R., under the stage. The performance being over, the trio returned to the dressing room to change clothing, wash, etc. Now D. and R. commenced to wrangle. Angry words and vile and slanderous epithets followed. Nosey was hurrying on his pants at a rapid rate. A fight was brewing; the door locked. Nosey begged them to let him out. The key was lost. The lights went out. D. and R. pitched into one another. Nosey "went to grass" by mistake!

"Murder!" cried Nosey, "they have torn my only pantaloons off!"

A sock-dolager on the lug of Nosey sent him head foremost into a bucket of dirty water (another mistake!). Murder was called very lustily by the prompter. The door was broken open by the carpenters and what a sight was presented! The belligerents were puffing and blowing but, strange to say, had not received even a scratch. But the unfortunate Nosey looked quite forlorn and "groggy." His left ogle was closed and his pants hung in ribbons. D. and R. agreed to take a drink and shake hands. Old "Phil" was invited to a pull, as he had acted impartially as second to both the men. D. and R. kept their secret and Nosey was never posted or had the slightest suspicion but the fight was a genuine one. All he blamed them for was their making so many mistaken blows.

The last days of the North Pearl Street Amphitheatre led to rather an up hill business. A Mr. Davis was manager, I believe. At the grand finale, Old Turnbull, father of Julia, the danseuse, produced an abolition drama full of woolly-headism. I have forgotten the name of the piece. It was quite affecting, however; the author himself cried in some of the most tender points. It had a fine run of---one evening. For some cause or other, the manager on the next evening was obliged, as he said, to dismiss the audience in consequence of some of the artists rebelling and refusing to play. While the manager was making this moving speech, the ticket seller smelt a good sized rat and, there being just $18 due him, he blew out the lights in the office and vamoosed with all the funds, $18, all in small change. The manager threw himself upon the kind indulgence of the audience and informed them that they could step to the box office and have the money refunded them. The ticket seller was *non est* and a free fight was the result. The chandelier was broken, as well as the manager, who made his escape through a sewer. The scene ended by old John Meigs, high constable, and his posse capturing some dozen "Canawlers" and two soldiers from the rendezvous. The old theatre soon wound up its earthly career.

Bill Lawson was engaged here about this time. He came to this country as ringmaster with West in 1816. He was a fine looking man. He could neither read nor write, yet he could play the part of a sailor in excellent style. His Mat Mizzen was the best ever produced on the American stage in that day. He played Joe Standfast equally well in "The Turnpike Gate." Bill was the first victim to the cholera in the summer of 1832. He died in a wretched cellar in Catherine Street, New York. Poor Bill. His worst enemy was rum. *Transeat in exemplum.*

Near the same locality and equally as miserably, Miss Emery (Mrs. Burroughs), the great English tragic actress, died. Her acting of Bianca was a most thrilling picture. Her untimely end was much regretted.

In the orchestra of the old North Pearl Street Amphitheatre was to be seen and heard a remarkable personage. His name was Paddy Burns and he was one of the best Kent buglers of that day. Paddy, of course, was a son of the Emerald Isle. He was in the British service most of his days; his regiment was stationed opposite Fort Niagara, Canada. Paddy had made up his mind "solid," as he said, to Yankee-ize himself, as Uncle Sam's dominions were only on the opposite side of Niagara River, some nine or ten miles below Niagara Falls. Burns was suspected and was consequently watched very closely; so that an attempt to escape was a dangerous experiment. But he tried it and succeeded. On one fine morning, Paddy had an innocent confab with the sentinel, whose station was near the bank of the river. A few drops of the "crather" cemented the bonds of friendship close as wax. The sentinel got three sheets in the wind, while Paddy Burns was as sober as the Pope. He managed to pour some of the liquor into the vigilant soldier's gun, unperceived. Paddy then retired from the presence of his friend, behind a rock, tied his bugle on his neck and plunged into the river and swam a great distance from the shore before he was discovered. The alarm was given, the sentinels gun flashed in the pan, and Paddy arrived safe in the "Land of the Free and the Home of the Brave," amid the loud huzzas of the spectators on the American shore, who had watched the proceedings with the most intense anxiety. Burns then mounted a high elevation and played "Yankee Doodle" and "Hail Columbia" in the very teeth of John Bull. Paddy was liked by all who knew him. He died in Ohio.

X

John May, the clown, was admitted to the insane department of Blockley's Almshouse, Philadelphia, May 13th, 1854, where he died June 12th of the same year. He was struck on the head out West by a stone, from the effects of which he lost his memory and was unable to perform for some time. He was a very worthy man, strictly temperate and of a very lively wit. His old companions supported him until it was found that he could receive better nursing and attention at Blockley, where he was sent. John was born in Orange County, state of New York, September 7th, 1816. When a boy he was apprenticed to a tailor but, having a soul immeasurably above buttons and feeling no desire to become distinguished as a knight of the shears, he soon cut the business and we find him connected with a circus company, for which profession he had always entertained a predilection. From that day his course was one of continued honor and profit, he having amassed quite a handsome competency in his business and attained a reputation second to none of his rivals. In 1844, he visited Europe professionally and performed with éclat at all the principal cities of England, France, Spain, etc. He extended his travels into Africa and subsequently visited South America. The announcement of Mr. May's name upon the bills was sure to secure a full house.

In private life he was richly esteemed for his many virtues, proverbial liberality and excellence of heart. Having traveled much, he had accumulated a valuable fund of information and anecdote and was always as pleasing and attractive in private conversation as in a professional capacity. His first appearance before a Philadelphia audience took place March 19th, 1845, at the Old National Theatre as Jonathan in "The Heroic Struggle of 1776." Poor Jack! "We could have spared a better man." *Memoria in Eterna.*

Mary Ann Cooke, daughter of William Cooke, equestrian, died at Halifax, Yorkshire, England, from the effects of a severe accident. She was thrown from her horse against the side of the ring while performing and her skull fractured. She was but eleven years old but a great favorite.

William Harrington, equestrian, a native of Boston, died at Milledgeville, Ga., November 4, 1835, aged thirty-one. Some time previous to his death he was in St. Louis with Rockwell's Circus and, having on a certain occasion fallen from his horse, he was considered deranged. While in St. Louis he made several attempts to kill himself by discharging a revolver through his left cheek. He then shot himself through the head, a ball being in the pistol each time. He ran into the entry of the hotel with the blood streaming down his face. Upon some friends attempting to stop him, he discharged a bullet at them but missed them. He then invited a friend to see him shoot himself and, seating himself on a pile of wood, deliberately lodged the ball in his brain....

James McFarland, attached to Spalding & Rogers' Circus Company, met with his death while traveling in western Missouri at the hands of a Mr. Roberts, landlord of a hotel in Liberty, Missouri. It seems that Spalding & Rogers and North's company were both to perform in Liberty on the same day. Mlle. Costello, formerly Mrs. McFarland, was with North's company. The landlord had received positive orders from North not to allow anyone to see the lady and to keep a strict watch over her. McFarland, learning that his wife was there, called and demanded of the landlord permission to see her. He refused. Then McFarland proceeded upstairs and the landlord, seizing a bowie-knife, put after him. Hard words ensued and, drawing their weapons simultaneously, a desperate fight occurred. McFarland was stabbed in the neck, separating the jugular vein, and was also cut several times in the body. He died in three minutes. The deceased drew his weapon and fired one load but missed his antagonist. Every attempt to fire subsequently was ineffectual from the caps snapping. The burial of the deceased took place the following day and was attended by all the members of Spalding & Rogers' company. *Ira Furor brevis est.*

Sol J. Lipman died in Cincinnati November 2 [just passed], aged forty-four. He was long and favorably known as clown. Sol was a native of Philadelphia and followed the vocation of clown for upwards of thirty years. He was full of eccentricity and fun, a man of honor and a warm friend. *Sit tibi terra levis.*

Jack Whittaker, this celebrated equestrian, died in April, 1847. He was at Vera Cruz and on the bloody field of Cerro Gordo, where he escaped in safety, though he left his mark on the body of many a greaser. He was afterwards wounded in a skirmish with a guerrilla party and taken to the hospital. He had nearly recovered from his wounds when he fell a victim to camp fever. His last words were:

"Boys, I've rode my last act. It was my best engagement and my last. Give always your horse a loose rein but never desert your flag!" Green be the turf above thee, glorious Jack.

James Stokes, slack wire vaulter, was killed by the Cherokee Indians while traveling on foot to Montgomery, Ala., in 1833. He was an Englishman of West's company.

Robert Lowry, for many years a clown, died at Dr. Stone's Hospital, New Orleans, of consumption in 1840.

Ivan Showeriskey, noted for his slack rope performance of suspending himself by one heel and then, while a shriek arose from the females comprising the audience, he would plunge into the air with a "jerk" sufficient to break the bones of a common man. While he was swinging by his heel in Baltimore in 1836, the rope affixed to the heel and attached to the large cord, suddenly broke and he plunged head foremost to the earth, upon which he alighted senseless. He had his leg amputated and shortly after died.

Frank Brower, clown, was born in Baltimore. The appearance of Frank in the ring is the cue for mirth; and his jests, always chaste and original, are such as would make a stoic hold his sides. I have spent many an hour listening to the laughter-provoking jests of Uncle Frank and must confess that, as a clown, I think he has but few equals.

Mme. Louisa Brower, formerly Louisa Howard, maiden name Banks, was born in Baltimore, Md. This celebrated and wonderful equestrienne received a greater amount of sincere, unbought and enthusiastic applause than was ever awarded to any person who has attempted the daring and heroic art which she practiced. Her unrivaled grace and astounding daring have been themes of eulogium, astonishment and admiration in all of the more populous cities of Europe. She is the only equestrienne, who ever graced this country, who rides with the grace, daring and elegance taught only by the Parisian schools; and she is acknowledged to have no superior in any part of the world. She is at present living in Philadelphia, enjoying her *Otium cum-dignitate*.

Ira Cole, circus manager and famous wrestler in his day, [was] born in the state of New York.

William Hyers, a clown of some merit, [was] born in Baltimore and died in Philadelphia in 1856.

Robert Williams, brought to this country by Cooke from England in 1837, was still living in 1858.

George Sergeant, an excellent equestrian of his day, was born in New York.

George Sweet, equestrian and tight rope performer attached to Bowery Amphitheatre, Buffalo, threw himself from the third story of the Eagle Tavern. He had for several days been laboring under a species of insanity and attempted to make away with himself by taking opium.

Noel E. Waring died at New Orleans, February, 1854. He was extensively known as manager of circuses and menageries throughout the United States. He was highly esteemed by all who had the pleasure of his acquaintance. He possessed a good heart and had all the fine feelings that characterize the philanthropist and the friend in need. His memory should be held in the highest estimation and cherished with affection and respect. *Amicus humuni generis.*

Pepin's Circus disbanded forever at Nashville in 1829. The only members of that company now living are Peter Coty and James Burt. Coty was known at the Walnut Street Circus in 1816 as the gay young American rider. He was married to Miss Payne at Charleston, S.C., in 1829. She is now living in Australia. Charles Durang, in his reminiscences, says he married a daughter of Manfreds. This is an error. The last accounts of Coty was that he was a homeless wanderer, old and infirm, but both honest and temperate. *Non compos mentis.*

Burt is at present living in Philadelphia, looking as young and as fresh an a fighting cock and withal a gentleman. *A capite ad calcem.*

Mr. James Raymond, the well known circus manager, died at his residence at Carmel, N.Y., in 1854. He left property valued at $1,500,000. Part of it was the Broadway Theatre, New York.

John Jackson (right name John McIllway), a slack rope performer, was born in Philadelphia; died in Columbus, Ga., in 1843.

J. H. Stickney was born in Boston [and] died at New Orleans.

W. Waterman [was] born in Rhode Island.

John Conklin was born in Cincinnati, where he died in 1838 from the effects of a fall while riding two horses.

Archibald Madden, clown, [was] born in Williamsburg, N.Y.

William Langley, son of Langley of Lailson's Circus, cut his throat at Charleston, S.C., in 1849, during a fit of *mania a potu.* His mother was quite wealthy and he had retired from the circus many years before his death. He was engaged with Sizer's Circus, a wandering troupe through Alabama, Florida, etc., most of his life. Every member of this troupe have retired to the tomb of the Capulets. The last I saw of them was at Clairborn, Ala., in 1836. *Ad finum.*

George Blythe, born in England, was engaged by Stephen Price as director of the Walnut Street Theatre and Circus,

Philadelphia, where he made his first appearance in America on the opening night, May 1st, 1823. He was formerly director of Astley's Amphitheatre, London. [He] retired from the profession and opened a porter house on Staten Island, N.Y., where he died in 1836.

W. F. Wallett, the unrivaled and celebrated clown, was born in England. He made his first appearance in America in New York. On the 17th of December, 1849, he appeared in Philadelphia at the National Circus. [His] first appeared on the stage as an actor [was] December 11, 1852, as Duke Aranza at the Chestnut, Philadelphia, for the benefit of Lysander Thompson.

Miss Sallie Stickney, this beautiful and accomplished equestrienne, has attracted a great deal of attention and comment; and the opinion is that she is one of the best female riders we have in the country. Certainly, if her youth and her talents are considered, she is without a rival in the country. In her "Principal Act," leaping, cutting, pirouetting and one-foot riding, she is very fine. She bears herself with a grace and dignity, a charm of manner, a frank, ladylike becoming ease and assurance that is positively irresistible. She jumps most gracefully and with great intrepidity; and no woman in the arena can ride on the bareback with the same degree of certainty and ease. She is a Philadelphian by birth and has been in the ring ever since she could walk.

John "Grimaldi" Wells, the clown, died in Philadelphia, April, 1852. Three of his daughters are at present in the profession. Mary Ann is the wife of Frank Whittaker, the best ringmaster in the country. Amelia was one of the daring "racers" of the Hippodrome. She is at present the wife of Robert Butler, low comedian, and is engaged at one of the saloons on Broadway, New York, as a vocalist. Miss Louisa was the danseuse at the National, Philadelphia. She is a thoroughly educated artiste, dances with grace and finish, and has made great progress of late years.

George Yeaman was born in Scotland. He came to the States with J. West in 1816. He was well known under the cognomen of "The Flying Horseman." [He] died, much regretted, at Concord, N.C., November 7th, 1827.

Dan Rice, the "humorist," was born in New York in the year 1822. He got his first glimpse of the elephant in his native city and, emigrating early in life to Pittsburgh and the far West, had ample chance to study human nature in all its phases. His intellect is fine, his perceptive powers acute, his fancy fertile, his judgment sound, and his imitations great. He is a wonderful example of what a man can effect by determination. He has met with every vicissitude which can befall an adventurer. His triumphs in training animals surpass those of any mortal in the world. His horse "Excelsior," he endowed with intellect, whilst he absolutely taught his elephant to walk a tight rope. His "mules" are great comedians. The high tone which has marked Mr. Rice's course and the unbending determination with which he conducts his entertainments reflect upon him great credit.

INDEX

INDEX